Exper

Emteaz

methuen | drama

LONDON • NEW YORK • OXFORD • NEW DELHI • SYDNEY

METHUEN DRAMA
Bloomsbury Publishing Plc
50 Bedford Square, London, WC1B 3DP, UK
1385 Broadway, New York, NY 10018, USA
29 Earlsfort Terrace, Dublin 2, Ireland.

BLOOMSBURY, METHUEN DRAMA and the Methuen
Drama logo are trademarks of Bloomsbury Publishing Plc.

First published in Great Britain 2024

A catalogue record for this book is available from the British Library.

A catalog record for this book is available from the Library of Congress.

ISBN: PB: 978-1-3505-5361-3
ePDF: 978-1-3505-5363-7
eBook: 978-1-3505-5362-0

Series: Modern Plays.

Typeset by Mark Heslington Ltd, Scarborough, North Yorkshire
Printed and bound in Great Britain.

To find out more about our authors and books visit
www.bloomsbury.com and sign up for our newsletters.

THE ROYAL COURT THEATRE PRESENTS

Expendable

By Emteaz Hussain

Expendable was first performed at The Royal Court Theatre Upstairs, Sloane Square on 21 November 2024.

Expendable

By Emteaz Hussain

Cast (in alphabetical order):
Jade Steel **Maya Bartley O'Dea**
Zara Sharif **Avita Jay**
Yasmin Sharif **Lena Kaur**
Raheel Sharif **Gurjeet Singh**
Sofia Sharif **Humera Syed**

Writer **Emteaz Hussain**
Director **Esther Richardson**
Designer **Natasha Jenkins**
Lighting Designer **Azusa Ono**
Dramaturg **Nazli Tabatabai-Khatambakhsh**
Sound Designer **Arun Ghosh**
Movement Director **Ayesha Fazal**
Casting Director **Nadine Rennie**
Costume Supervisor **Evelien Van Camp**
Design Associate **Helen Hebert**
Design Associate **Nate Gibson**
Voice and Accent Coach **Gurkiran Kaur**
Stage Manager **Jessica Thanki**
Stage Manager **Tanith MacKenzie**
Deputy Stage Manager **Aiman Bandali**
Stage Management Placement **Rosie Fleming**
Wellbeing Specialist **Shalina Litt**

From the Royal Court, on this production:

Executive Producer **Steven Atkinson**
Production Manager **Zara Drohan**
Lighting Supervisor **Lucinda Plummer**
Lighting Programmer **Lizzie Skellett**
Lead Producer **Ralph Thompson**
Company Manager **Mica Taylor**

Emteaz Hussain is the recipient of The Clare McIntyre Bursary.

The Royal Court and Stage Management wish to thank the following for their help with this production:
RADA, Lamda & National Theatre Prop Hire.

Emteaz Hussain (Writer)

For the Royal Court:
Living Newspaper Edition 2.

Other theatres include: **Still Life (Nottingham Playhouse); Social Distancing (Kali/Online); Crongton Knights, Outsiders (Pilot/UK Tour); Blood (& UK Tour), Sweet Cider (& Arcola) (Tamasha); Etching (The Break).**

Aiman Bandali
(Deputy Stage Manager)

For the Royal Court: **Word-Play.**

Other theatres include: **Hakawatis: The Women of the Arabian Nights (Sam Wanamaker Playhouse); Peanut Butter and Blueberries, The Darkest Part of the Night (Kiln); The Comeuppance (Almeida); The Bolds, The Three Billy Goats Gruff (Unicorn); Scandaltown (Lyric); My Brother's Keeper (Theatre503); A Midsummers Night Dream (Regents Park); Dick Whittington and his Cat (Lighthouse, Poole); Uncle Vanya, I & You (Hampstead); Don Carlos, Love Steals us from Loneliness, Rules for Living (Carne Studio); New England (Linbury Studio); Little Shop of Horrors, Earthquakes in London, The Cherry Orchard, Three Days in the Country, Twelfth Night, The River and The Mountain (Sainsbury Theatre).**

Maya Bartley O'Dea (Jade Steel)

Theatre includes: **Maryland, Punk Rock (Stratford East); Northern Girls (Pilot).**

Film includes: **Once Upon a Riot, The Cake Craze, You're a long time dead.**

Maya also co-runs Forbes 30 under 30

production company 'Broken Flames', which has a focus on mental health and how this is portrayed in the media.

Evelien Van Camp
(Costume Supervisor)

Theatre includes: **Rock'n Roll, Reykjavik (Hampstead); The Forsyte Saga (Park); The Circle, The Swell, Suite in Three Keys (Orange Tree); My Uncle is not Pablo Escobar (Brixton House); Marie Curie (Charing Cross).**

Opera includes: **Dead Man Walking (Guildhall); Orfeo (Longborough Festival Opera); Albert Herring, Barber of Seville (Clonter Opera); Carmen (Waterperry Opera Festival); Sir John in Love (British Youth Opera).**

Film includes: **The Expendables 4, Pretty Red Dress, Original Skin.**

Rosie Fleming (Stage Management Placement)

Theatre includes: **Twelfth Night, Anatomy of a Suicide, Mirandolina, Light Falls, The Tempest, MA Lab Red and Blue Shows (RADA).**

Ayesha Fazal (Movement Director)

Movement direction for theatre includes: **Run Rebel (Mercury/Tour); A Song For Ella Grey (Northern Stage/Tour); Firewall (Derby/Tour).**

Arun Ghosh (Sound Designer)

Theatre includes: **Great Expectations, Hobson's Choice, Antigone, The Tempest, Volpone (Royal Exchange); Closer, A Doll's House (Lyric); A Little Princess (Theatre By The Lake); Let's Build (Polka); Much Ado About Nothing, Arms and the Man, Dishoom!, Deranged Marriage, Coming Up (Watford Palace); The Bone Sparrow, Noughts and Crosses (Pilot); Lions and Tigers (Globe); Approaching Empty, Made in India, Blood, My Name Is..., Child of the Divide (Tamasha); Tagore's Women, The Husbands, Mustafa (Kali); Nothello, Under the Umbrella, Red Snapper (Belgrade); Indian Ink (Salisbury Playhouse); Kabbadi Kabbadi Kabbadi (Mercury); Bystanders, Glasshouse, Life Ain't No Musical (Cardboard Citizens); Storm (Contact); Arabian Nights (Manchester Library); And Did Those Feet (Octagon); Crazy Masala Club (Peshwar); The Mystery Show (Little Angel); The Snow Queen, London Eye Mystery, The Wolf, the Duck and the Mouse (Unicorn); The Jungle Book (Royal and Derngate); Big Sister Little Brother (Spark); The House of Inbetween (Stratford East); Run Sister Run (Paines Plough & Crucible).**

Dance includes: **Poems and Tiger Eggs, Tir (Ballet Cymru); Songs of the City (Akademi); A Handful of Dust (Rich Mix/Serious); Fading Contact, The Art of Travel (Kadam); Saptarishi, Faith in the City, Reach (Chaturangan).**

Opera includes: **The Rake's Progress (Nitro/Royal Opera House).**

Television includes: **Dream Factory, Rappin' at the Royal.**

Film includes: **Everywhere and Nowhere, Nothing Like Chocolate, Prantik, Forest of Humans, The Adventures of Prince Achmed.**

Radio includes: **Evening Conversations, The Healing Pool, Ek Awaaz, The Secret Garden.**

Awards include: **Parliamentary Jazz Award - Jazz Instrumentalist of the Year.**

Helen Hebert (Design Associate)

Theatre includes: **The Way of the World (Aberystwyth University); Sh*t Happens (Camden Peoples); Little Miss Burden (Bunker); Les Absent.e.s (El Duende); Barefaced (Chelsea); Salt (Theatre 503); Home, Is God Is (LAMDA).**

Dance includes: **The Monocle (Rendez-Vous Dance).**

Opera as associate designer includes: **The Dialogue of the Carmelites (Liege); Alcina (Wuppertal); The Handmaid's Tale (San Francisco).**

Film includes: **Dues, Waving, This Man.**

Natasha Jenkins (Designer)

Theatre design includes: **An Enemy of the People (West End); LOVE (National/Park Avenue Armory/Odéon-Théâtre de l'Europe/Wiener Festwochen); Danton Reloaded (Thalia Theater); The Beauty Queen of Leenane (By The Lake); Professor Bernhardi (Freiburg); Scissors (Sheffield); Une mort dans la famille (Odéon-Théâtre de l'Europe); Faith, Hope and Charity (National/Wiener Festwochen/European Tour); Eine Griechische Trilogie (Berliner Ensemble); Beyond Caring (National/The Yard/Schaubühne/Tour); Uncle Vanya (HOME Manchester); The High Table (Bush); In Basildon (Queens Hornchurch); Richard III (Perth); Clockwork Canaries (Drum Plymouth); Stand By (Utter); The Whip Hand (National of Scotland/Traverse), 20b (&Tour), (Birmingham Rep); Monstrous Bodies (Dundee Rep); Disney's Freaky Friday (Arts Ed); Romeo and Juliet (RADA); Damned Rebel Bitches (Poorboy Scottish Tour).**

Television design includes: **Love.**

Film design includes: **7 Keys, A Sharp Arrow, The Everlasting Club and Ma'am, Myrtle and Annekas Problems, Loose Ends, Forgiveness, Here We Are.**

Music video design includes: **Anywhere But Here (Rag'n'Bone Man & P!nk).**

Avita Jay (Zara Sharif)

Theatre includes: **A Tupperware of Ashes (National); The Secret Garden (Regent's Park); The Empress, Falkland Sound, The Comedy of Errors, The Winter's Tale (RSC); Jinnistan (Traverse); Favour (Bush); The Lovely Bones (Birmingham Rep); Billionaire Boy (NST Theatre/Tour); The Secret Garden (York Theatre Royal); The Jungle Book (Tour); Bottled Up (Lyric); Bring on the Bollywood (Tour); We're Stuck (Shoreditch Town Hall/Tour); Rapunzel, Warde Street (Park); Pioneer (Crucible/Tour); Unsung (Wilton's Music Hall); The Merry Wives of Windsor (Tour); Sunday Morning at the Centre of the World (Southwark); Spare (New Diorama).**

Television includes: **Casualty, Doctors, The Good Ship Murder, Emmerdale, Silent Witness, Coronation Street, L8R.**

Film includes: **By Any Other Name, The Rezort, London, Paris, New York, Twenty8K.**

Other: **Avita also narrates audiobooks for Audible and works for the charity, InterAct Stroke Support.**

Nate Gibson (Design Associate)

Theatre includes: **The Way of the World, Almost Maine (Alfred University); Macbeth (Cordial Productions); NSFW, Realism, Holes in the Skin, A Bright New Boise, Pomona, Clybourne Park (Lamda).**

Dance includes: **Murder My Sweet! (National Dance Company Wales); The Monocle (Rendez-Vous Dance); Opera includes A Christmas Carol (Welsh National Opera & Haydn Foundation);**

Simplicius Simplicissimus, L'Incoronazione di Poppea, Anna Bolena, The Cunning Little Vixen, Die Tote Stadt, L'Orfeo, The Fairy Queen (Longborough Festival Opera); The Marriage of Figaro, Don Giovanni (Clonter Farm Opera); The Emperor of Atlantis (Loud Crowd); Sir John in Love (British Youth Opera); Maria de Rudenz (Gothic Opera).

Film includes: **Myrtle, Anywhere Away From Here, Mummy's Present.**

Lena Kaur (Yasmin Sharif)

For the Royal Court: **Living Archive.**
Theatre includes: **The Cat and the Canary (Chichester Festival/Told by an Idiot), Betty! A Sort of Musical, The Ghost Train (& Told by an Idiot), (Royal Exchange); The Last Testament of Lillian Bilocca (Hull Truck); Earthworks, Myth, The Two Noble Kinsmen, The Rover, Seven Acts of Mercy (RSC); Around the World in 80 Days (St James Theatre); Treasure Island (National); Thursday (ETT/Australian tour); Sisters (Sheffield Theatres); Rubina (Birmingham Rep); The Sky's The Limit (Old Vic); Free World (Contact); Silent Cry (West Yorkshire Playhouse).**

Television includes: **I, Jack Wright, Happy Valley, Stargazing, Justin's House, Doctors, Dani's Castle, Prisoners' Wives, Torchwood, Emmerdale, Speechless, Hollyoaks, Scallywagga, Torn.**

Radio includes: **Reality Check, Silver Street, Maps for Lost Lovers.**

Film includes: **The Radleys.**

Gurkiran Kaur
(Voice and Accent Coach)

For the Royal Court: **Dugzi Days**

Theatre includes: **A Tupperware of Ashes (National); Ghost Stories by Candlelight (High Tide); King Troll (Kali & New Diorama); Peanut Butter & Blueberries (Kiln); Dylan Mulvaney: FAGHAG (Soho); Refugee! (62**

Gladstone Street); The Secret Garden (Regents Park); Sweat, Great Expectations (Royal Exchange); The Buddha of Surburbia. Falkland Sounds, The Empress (RSC); Frankie Goes To Bollywood (Watford Palace); Wolves On Road, The Real Ones, The Cord, A Playlist For The Revolution, Paradise Now, The P Word, Favour, Red Pitch (&West End), (Bush); This Much I Know, Lotus Beauty (Hampstead); The Enormous Crocodile: The Musical (Leeds Playhouse); A Poem For Rabia (Tarragon Theatre); Brassic FM (Gate); I Wanna Be Yours (Melbourne Theatre); Wuthering Heights, Unexpected Twist (Royal & Derngate); Anansi The Spider, Marvin's Binoculars (Unicorn); I Wonder If..., Chasing Hares, Best of Enemies (Young Vic); A Dead Body In Taos (Fuel); Silence (Donmar); The Best Exotic Marigold Hotel (West End); Finding Home (Curve); The Climbers (Theatre by The Lake); Offside (Futures Theatre); Henry VIII (Globe); Queens of Sheba (Soho); How To Save The Planet When You're A Young Carer & Broke (Roundhouse); NW Trilogy (Kiln); Extinct (Stratford East).

Television includes: **Good Karma Hospital, Hotel Portofino.**

Tanith MacKenzie (Stage Manager)

Theatre includes: Withnail & I, The Lion the Witch and the Wardrobe, The Play What I Wrote (Birmingham Rep); 2:22 A Ghost Story, The Upstart Crow (West End); Dreamboats & Petticoats, Soul Sister (Bill Kenwright); Vanara (Giovanna Romagnoli/Mark Goucher Productions); A Taste of Honey, Macbeth, Hedda Gabler (National/Tour); The Be All and End All (York Theatre Royal); An Improbable Musical (& Improbable), The Lion the Witch and the Wardrobe, Honk: The Ugly Duckling Musical, Orvin: Champion of Champions, Just Between Ourselves, The Vikings and Darwin, The Wizard of Oz, Zombie Prom, Ubu Roi, Burying Your Brother in the

Pavement, Frankenstein, 101 Dalmatians, The Way of the World, Soap, Pinocchio (Royal & Derngate).

Opera includes: **Tamerlano, Manon Lescaut, Belshazzar, Il Ritourno d'Ulisse in Patria (The Grange Festival).**

Azusa Ono (Lighting Designer)

Theatre includes: **The Spy Who Came In From The Cold (Chichester Festival); A Mirror (West End & Almeida); Grenfell in the words of survivors (National and St. Ann's Warehouse); Romeo & Juliet (Royal Exchange); Macbeth (Shakespeare North and International tour); Henry V (Sam Wanamaker/Tour); Watch on the Rhine, A Doll's House, Part 2 (Donmar); Much Ado About Nothing (RSC); Can I Live?, Copyright Christmas (Barbican); Walden (Harold Pinter); Blue Orange, Concubine (Birmingham Rep); Lao Can Impression, Yvette (Southbank Centre); Love Lies Bleeding (The Print Room); Thick As Thieves (Clean Break/Tour); Abandon (Lyric); Smack That (Barbican/Tour); Effigies of Wickedness (Gate); Cuttin' It (Young Vic/Tour); Darkness Darkness (Nottingham Playhouse); Peddling (New York 59E59/Tour); We Are Proud...(Bush); The Love Song of Alfred J Hitchcock (Curve Leicester/Tour).**

Opera includes: **The Magic Flute (Nevill Holt Festival Opera); Kairos Opera (V&A Museum).**

Other projects include: **COP27 Health Pavilion (Sharm El Sheikh); The Sleeping Tree (Brighton Dome); Aurora (Toxteth Water Reservoir Liverpool); Tate Live Exhibition – Joan Jonas (Tate).**

Esther Richardson (Director)

Esther is currently the Artistic Director of Pilot Theatre company based in York, UK.

Theatre includes: **Brighton Rock (& York Theatre Royal), Noughts and Crosses, The Bone Sparrow, Crongton Knights (& Derby/Belgrade Coventry/Colchester Mercury/York Theatre Royal), A Song For Ella Grey, Traitor (& Teatret Vårt), (Pilot); Blood (Tamasha/Belgrade Coventry); Private Lives (Mercury); How to Breathe, Breaking the Silence (Nottingham Playhouse); The Glee Club (Cast in Doncaster); Sky Bus, Be My Baby, A Kind of Alaska, The Dumb Waiter, Wasteland (& New Perspectives), Bones (& Fifth Word) (Derby Live); Town (Royal and Derngate, Northampton); Dancehall (Theatre du Campagnol); Everything Must Go! (Soho); Earl of Mo'Bay (Theatre Writing Partnership).**

Film includes: **The Summer Child, The Cake, Wings.**

Nadine Rennie (Casting Director)

Theatre includes: **Miracle on 34th Street (HOME Manchester); Pig Heart Boy (Unicorn/ tour); Wish You Were Here (Gate); The Flea (Yard); My Mother's Funeral: The Show, Run Sister Run (Paines Plough); Miss Julie, Leaves of Glass (Park); Dead Girls Rising (Silent Uproar); He Said She Said, Es & Flo (&WMC), (Kiln); Wreckage, Breeding (King's Head); Further Than The Furthest Thing (Minack); SHED: Exploded View (Royal Exchange); Bacon (Finborough); Super High Resolution, The Ministry of Lesbian Affairs (Soho); Britannicus (Lyric); The Breach (Hampstead); Little Baby Jesus (Orange Tree); The Last King of Scotland, Typical Girls, We Could All Be Perfect (Sheffield Theatres); There Are No Beginnings (Leeds).**

Prior to going Freelance, Nadine was in-house Casting Director at Soho Theatre for over fifteen years.

Gurjeet Singh (Raheel Sharif)

Theatre includes: **No Pay? No Way!, Wuthering Heights, Hobson's Choice (Royal Exchange); East is East (Birmingham Rep/National), Dara (National); The Importance of Being Earnest (Lawrence Batley Theatre/The Dukes); The Manchester Project at Christmas, On Corporation Street (HOME); A Christmas Carol (Hull Truck); Goth Weekend (Newcastle Live); The Rise and Fall of Little Voice (Stephen Joseph Theatre).**

Television includes: **Hotel Portofino, Mrs Sidhu Investigates, Ackley Bridge, The Bay, Three Girls, Broken Biscuits.**

Radio includes: **Southall Uprising, Whose Baby.**

Humera Syed (Sofia Sharif)

Theatre includes: **Peanut Butter & Blueberries (Kiln); Great Expectations (Royal Exchange); FAITH (RSC/Coventry City of Culture); The Village (Stratford East); The Arabian Nights (Royal Lyceum Theatre); Anita and Me (Tour).**

Television includes: **The Stranger, Hullraisers.**

Radio includes: **Tumanbay.**

Nazli Tabatabai-Khatambakhsh (Dramaturg)

Theatre includes as director and dramaturg: **The Tempest (Royal Central School of Speech and Drama).**

Theatre includes as director: **Tiger Mum, I'm Not Here (Traverse); Here They Come (Artistic Directors of the Future at Bush); Made in England, SOLD (Talawa); SILK (Dance City); A Little Hero (QWERK); Tales of the Arabian Nights (Theatre Workshop Edinburgh); Bad Medicine (Derby Theatre).**

Theatre includes as writer: **Medea on the Mic (Play, Pie and a Pint); Paper Dolls (Northern Stage); Congress (All The Queens Men); Safe Passage (CURVE).**

Theatre includes as actor: **White Rabbit, Red Rabbit, BLANK (Aurora Nova); Horizontal Collaboration (Fire Exit); Theatre Uncut (Paines Plough Roundabout).**

Theatre includes as dramaturg: **Mercy (Tamasha); And Then The Day Came (Peter Groom).**

Dance includes as dramaturg: **Sense of an Ending (Company of Others).**

Opera includes as librettist: **TIDE (Britten Pears); Leonard (Birmingham Opera Company); My Name Is... (Oxford Lieder); One Thousand Threads (National Youth Choir).**
Opera includes as a practice-based researcher: **Welsh Iranian Opera Symposium (Welsh National Opera).**
Opera includes as an artist: **T'UQ (Royal Opera House).**
Opera includes as a director: **Rotten Kid (Milton Court Barbican).**

Film includes as director: **68 Months in Waiting.**
Film includes as writer: **Next of Kin.**

Radio includes as director: **Silver Street.**
Radio includes as producer: **Iranian Voices.**

Performance poetry includes: **Poet in the City (Wigmore Hall).**

Moderator and Facilitation includes: **IETM Aarhus Plenary, ISPA New York Congress.**

Awards include: **Amnesty International Commendation Award at Edinburgh Festival Fringe for Waiting Room.**

Jessica Thanki (Stage Manager)

For the Royal Court: **Inside Bitch R&D, Broken Dreams, Living Newspaper edition 4, Sound of The Underground.**

Other theatres include: **Bear Snores On, Every Leaf a Hallelujah, 101 Dalmatians (Regents Park); REHAB The Musical (Clive Black); Dracula: Mina's Reckoning (National Scotland); Famous Five (Theatr Clwyd/ Chichester Festival); The Lion, The Witch and The Wardrobe (Elliot and Harper); Mischief Movie Night (Mischief); Trailer Story (ETT); Gruffalo's Child (Tall Stories); We're Going on a Bear Hunt (Kenny Wax); Dragons, Gentle Giant (Bamboozle); Another Paradise, Behna, AD2050, Black-I, Gandhi and Coconuts, Tagore's Women, Mustafa, The Dishonored, Ready or Not, War Plays, Homing Birds (Kali); The Muddy Choir (Theatre Centre); Cathy (Cardboard Citizens); Clockwork Canaries (Theatre Royal Plymouth); Tales of Birbal (Mashi); Dea by Edward Bond (Sutton Theatre).**

THE ROYAL COURT THEATRE

The Royal Court Theatre is the writers' theatre. It is a leading force in world theatre for cultivating and supporting writers - undiscovered, emerging and established.

Since 1956, we have commissioned and produced hundreds of writers, from John Osborne to Mohamed-Zain Dada. Royal Court plays from every decade are now performed on stages and taught in classrooms and universities across the globe.

Through the writers, the Royal Court is at the forefront of creating restless, alert, provocative theatre about now. We open our doors to the unheard voices and free thinkers that, through their writing, change our way of seeing.

We strive to create an environment in which differing voices and opinions can co-exist. In current times, it is becoming increasingly difficult for writers to write what they want or need to write without fear, and we will do everything we can to rise above a narrowing of viewpoints.

Through all our work, we strive to inspire audiences and influence future writers with radical thinking and provocative discussion.

🐦 royalcourt f royalcourttheatre

Supported using public funding by
ARTS COUNCIL
ENGLAND

ROYAL COURT SUPPORTERS

Our incredible community of supporters makes it possible for us to achieve our mission of nurturing and platforming writers at every stage of their careers. Our supporters are part of our essential fabric – they help to give us the freedom to take bigger and bolder risks in our work, develop and empower new voices, and create world-class theatre that challenges and disrupts the theatre ecology.

To all our supporters, thank you. You help us to write the future.

PUBLIC FUNDING

CHARITABLE PARTNERS

The Common Humanity Arts Trust

BackstageTrust

COCKAYNE

T. S. ELIOT FOUNDATION

JERWOOD FOUNDATION

CORPORATE SPONSORS & SUPPORTERS

Aqua Financial Ltd
Cadogan
Concord Theatricals
Edwardian Hotels, London
NJA Ltd. – Core Values & Creative Management
Prime Time
Sustainable Wine Solutions
Walpole

CORPORATE MEMBERS
Bloomberg Philanthopies
Sloane Stanley

TRUSTS & FOUNDATIONS

Maria Björnson Memorial Fund
Martin Bowley Charitable Trust
Bruce Wake Charitable Trust
Chalk Cliff Trust
The Noël Coward Foundation
Cowley Charitable Foundation
The Davidson PlayGC Bursary
Garrick Charitable Trust
The Lynne Gagliano Writers' Award
The Harold Hyam Wingate Foundation
John Lyon's Charity
The Marlow Trust
Clare McIntyre's Bursary
Old Possum's Practical Trust
Richard Radcliffe Charitable Trust
Rose Foundation
The Royal Borough of Kensington & Chelsea Arts Grant
Royal Victoria Hall Foundation
Theatres Trust
The Thistle Trust
The Thompson Family Charitable Trust

INDIVIDUAL SUPPORTERS

Artistic Director's Circle

Eric Abraham
Katie Bradford
Jeremy & Becky Broome
Clyde Cooper
Debbie De Girolamo &
Ben Babcock
Dominique & Neal Gandhi
Lydia & Manfred Gorvy
David & Jean Grier
Charles Holloway OBE
Linda Keenan
Andrew Rodger and Ariana
Neumann
Jack Thorne & Rachel Mason
Sandra Treagus for
ATA Assoc. LTD
Anonymous

Writers' Circle

Chris & Alison Cabot
Cas Donald
Robyn Durie
Melanie J. Johnson
Nicola Kerr
Héloïse and
Duncan Matthews KC
Emma O'Donoghue
Maureen & Tony Wheeler
Anonymous

Directors' Circle

Piers Butler
Fiona Clements
Professor John Collinge
Julian & Ana Garel-Jones
Carol Hall
Dr Timothy Hyde
Anonymous

Platinum Circle

Moira Andreae
Tyler Bollier
Katie Bullivant
Beverley Buckingham
Anthony Burton CBE
Matthew Dean
Emily Fletcher
The Edwin Fox Foundation
Beverley Gee
Lucy and Spencer De Grey
Madeleine Hodgkin
Damien Hyland
Susanne Kapoor
David P Kaskel & Christopher
A Teano
Peter & Maria Kellner
Robert Ledger & Sally
Moulsdale
Frances Lynn
Mrs Janet Martin
Andrew McIver
Barbara Minto
Brian & Meredith Niles
Timothy Prager
Corinne Rooney
Anita Scott
Bhags Sharma
Sir Paul & Lady Ruddock
Dr Wendy Sigle
Brian Smith
James and Victoria Tanner
Mrs Caroline Thomas
Yannis Vasatis
Sir Robert & Lady Wilson
Anonymous

With thanks to our Silver and Gold Supporters, and our Friends and Good Friends, whose support we greatly appreciate.

Let's be friends. With benefits.

Our Friends and Good Friends are part of the fabric of the Royal Court. They help us to create world-class theatre, and in return they receive early access to our shows and a range of exclusive benefits.

Join today and become a part of our community.

Become a Friend (from £40 a year)

Benefits include:

- Priority Booking
- Advanced access to £15 Monday tickets
- 10% Bar & Kitchen discount (including Court in the Square)
- 10% off Royal Court playtexts

Become a Good Friend (from £95 a year)

In addition to the Friend benefits, our Good Friends also receive:

- Five complimentary playtexts for Royal Court productions
- An invitation for two to step behind the scenes of the Royal Court Theatre at a special event

Our Good Friends' membership also includes a voluntary donation. This extra support goes directly towards supporting our work and future, both on and off stage.

To become a Friend or a Good Friend, or to find out more about the different ways in which you can get involved, visit our website: royalcourttheatre. com/support-us

The English Stage Company at the Royal Court Theatre is a registered charity (No. 231242)

Expendable

*'I just think goodness is more interesting. Evil is
constant. You can think of different ways to murder
people, but you can do that at age five. But you have to
be an adult to consciously, deliberately be good – and
that's complicated.'*

Toni Morrison

Still for justice and deep love:
Amma, Abba
Zafar, Azar, Shahnaz, Shamshad
Rukhtaz & Gulnaz

Deepest thanks must go to all the survivors and workers who entrusted me with their experiences and stories. David Byrne and all at the Royal Court Theatre who have journeyed with me from both the past and present tenures. Special thanks to Shaista Gohir and the Muslim Women's Network. Zlakha Ahmed and Apna Haq. Gulnaz Hussain, Pooja Ghai and the indomitable shero that is Esther Richardson.

Characters

Zara Sharif, *British Pakistani, 42*
Yasmin Sharif, *British Pakistani, 44*
Sofia (**Zara**'s *daughter*), *British Pakistani, 18*
Voice/Jade Steel, *White British, 21*
Raheel (**Zara**'s *son*), *British Pakistani, 20*
[**Jamal** (**Yasmin**'s *son, offstage*), *Mixed Pakistani Jamaican, 21*]

[*text in brackets*] *indicate words not spoken*

. . . indicates active silence or that the character cannot express what they are thinking

/ denotes the overlapping of speech

Scene One

November 2011. Forestdale – deindustrialised town in northern England.

Monday afternoon. **Zara***'s busy messy kitchen.*

A small bowl full of peeled garlic cloves, and a larger bowl of sliced onions, are on a table with a pile of unpeeled onions next to them.

Zara *is standing carefully peeling one of the onions.*

Once she's finished peeling the outer skin she starts to slice – careful, deliberate, meditative.

A sudden loud knock at the front door – offstage.

Voice (*from behind the front door*)   Aunty Zara! . . . Aunty Zara! . . .

Zara *quickly runs and hides, knife still in hand.*

Knocking continues.

Voice   Aunty Zara, anyone in?

Zara *freezes.*

Voice   Aunty Zara . . . you there?

Zara   . . .

Voice   anyone there?

Loud, determined knocking again.

Voice   Aunty Zara . . .?

Raheel?

Sofia?

Zara   . . .

Voice   . . .

Voice   anyone in?

Voice *gives up. Pushes a slip of paper through the letterbox.*
Footsteps leave.

Zara *appears from behind the cupboard.*

Checks the kitchen window to see if they're coming around the back.
Reassured, she exits to the front of the house – offstage.

She returns with a slip of paper in her hand and a couple of
takeaway leaflets.

Takes a moment as she looks at the slip of paper: screws it up,
throws it in the bin, leaves the takeaway leaflets on the side.

Rechecking the kitchen window again to see if the coast is clear.
Relieved, she visibly relaxes.

Zara *looks for her mobile. Finds it. Begins to scroll. Presses a*
number. The phone dials. She waits. It answers:

Zara   it's just me.

Pause.

Zara   whaddya mean 'again'?

Pause.

y'still ant done it?

Pause.

pushing it a bit aren't ya, don't ya think?

Pause.

why wouldn't we be going, Khalda!? why you think that?

Beat.

why?

Longer pause.

Zara   but you *have* got four days left tho, think about it? it's
like plenty o' time isn't it . . .?

Pause.

Zara I can't come over now, can I? I've got the khatham, I told ya.

Pause.

who's this Mariam? I don't know her tho, do I?

Beat.

but you've got four *whole* days, four. whole. days. Khalda. that's like plenty of time, isn't it? if you start in a bit, then do a bit later, a bit tomorrow . . . we'll / come fri . . .

Pause.

Zara what do you mean y'gotta go?

Pause.

leave the teal one! juss do the indigo and the orange one . . .

Beat.

like I said, if you start in a bit, then tomorrow and . . .

Khalda cuts the call.

Zara hold on . . .

Beat.

shit!

Zara *redials, it goes straight to voicemail.* **Zara**, *frustrated, cuts the call.*

Zara *looks at her watch, decides to finish adding her prepared toppings to a pizza base. Slightly frantic now. She shoves the pizza in the oven.*

She moves back to the busy table to continue to slice the onion – frantic and peed off now.

She cuts her hand badly, drops the bowl of sliced onions all over the floor:

shit! shit! shit!

Runs to the sink as drops of blood fall onto her dress, runs the tap, sticks her hand under it.

Enter **Yasmin** *– through the back (kitchen) door – with a can of Red Bull, a copy of a newspaper under her arm, and a bunch of keys.*

Noticing the mess, blood, and **Zara's** *panic:*

Yasmin   what. the. actual. fuck, Zara!

Beat.

Zara   Yas!!

what y'doing 'ere!?

Yasmin   . . .

Zara   . . .

Yasmin *puts her can of Red Bull, newspaper and keys on the kitchen table, negotiating the mess, she approaches* **Zara** *in pain at the sink:*

Yasmin   show me?

Yasmin *looks at* **Zara's** *hand:*

ooh it's a bleeder . . .

your plasters?

Zara *points to the first aid kit.* **Yasmin** *goes to get the kit.*

Zara   . . . still got a key?

Yasmin   course, being discreet ennit . . .

Zara   dint tell me you /

Yasmin   called – no answer . . .

Yasmin *takes out a plaster/bandage, antiseptic from the first aid kit:*

texted – no answer . . .

Zara   oh y'know how it is . . . busy, busy ey?

no rest for the wicked as they say . . . no rest . . .

Yasmin *starts to clean* **Zara***'s wound:*

Zara   don't fuss . . . please . . . I'm alright, I am . . .

Yasmin *(looking around)*   looks like it . . .

Beat.

here . . . *(Showing TCP antiseptic.)*

Zara *winces, she takes the cotton pad off* **Yasmin** *to do herself, then puts it down:*

Yasmin   ya want an infection do ya?

I'm still yer big sister.

Yasmin*, persistent, puts some antiseptic onto another cotton pad and then gently taps the wound.*

Zara   ooowww! Yasmin! fffffffffffff – whoa!

Beat.

Yasmin   y'can swear y'know, no one's listening . . .

Zara   don't start, Yasmin, don't need it!

As the wound is dealt with:

Jamal, you've not brought him have you?

(Referring to the mess.) don't need to see all this.

Yasmin   just me.

saw them spilling onto the street.

Zara   . . .

Yasmin   kids outside. reminded me of us playing . . . it's like things don't change round here . . .

Zara   believe, things have changed round here.

Beat.

Yasmin   new kitchen?

Zara   yeah, had it done this year.

Beat.

Zara   your hair? looks good, shorter . . .?

Yasmin   . . .

Zara   suits you.

Yasmin   haven't got the patience for it these days.

Zara   y'not got work today?

Yasmin   your mobile . . . y'not answering . . . Zara?

Zara *busies herself: attempts but fails to start on the onions again due to her wound, starts tidying instead.*

Zara   you know how it is . . . with work n everything . . . I got two of 'em, growing bigguns, you've just got the one . . . keep my phone off most of the time.

Yasmin   where's Raheel? Sofe . . .?

Zara   out . . .

Yasmin   really!?

Beat.

how are they then? your two . . .

Zara   all of us . . . got to keep going . . . Sofe's at college, Raheel's working, I'm working . . . it's like Dory from *Finding Nemo* isn't it . . . just keep swimming, swimming, swimming . . . y'know *Finding Nemo* don't ya, Dory . . . just keep swimming, swimming, swimming . . .

Yasmin *referring to all the mess:*

Yasmin   feeding the five thousand are ya?

Zara   khatham tonight – year on dua.

everyone gets fed, don't they . . .

Yasmin   thought you'd take a break?

Zara khatam later, work trip tomorrow, shaadi on Sunday,
busy busy ey?

how long y'over for?

Yasmin a shaadi?!

Zara just for the day then?

Yasmin a shaadi?!

Zara Khalda, remember her? dressmaker from school.
year below you. she hasn't finished our outfits . . . proper let
me down . . .

Yasmin !

Zara I mean, she sez she thought we won't be going, why
won't we be going? I could kill her . . . why . . .? don't know
why she thought that . . .

Yasmin whose shaadi?

Zara three weeks she's had my fabric, can y'believe it, three
weeks! I'm telling her she's got four days, four, I mean four
'whole' days to get it done . . . redeem herself, plenty of time
. . . isn't it / like she could . . .

Yasmin whose shaadi tho, Zara?

Zara don't worry, y'won't know 'em. not close.

Sofia n me we'll be parked outside her house on friday, if she
pretends she's not in, I have this feeling.

Yasmin if they're not close d'ya have to go / tho'?

Zara course I have to go!

Beat.

thought you'd remember 'Khalda'. her and her sister both
married those brothers from Pakistan, y'know the one she
said had three nipples that time.

Yasmin course I remember Khalda!!

Zara   y'not been here in what . . . years . . . how long
y'staying for? must be two years is it, Yas? since we saw yer
. . .

Yasmin   like I tell yer, like I tell yer, when y'answer y'phone,
y'can always come to / Manchester.

Zara   divorced now, Khalda. tells me to try this other, use
this woman I've never met. why would I use someone I've
never met for shaadi outfits!! I mean shaadi outfits . . .! think
about it . . . shaadi outfits, someone I've never used before
for shaadi outfits . . .! think about it.

Yasmin   but of all the times /

Zara   can't believe she's just landed me in the lurch like this
. . . I mean, as if I wouldn't go . . . why wouldn't I go . . . don't
know why she thought that . . .

Yasmin   you don't have to go tho do ya.

Zara   said I'd go. I promised.

Beat.

a wedding that's been planned for over a year.

Yasmin *takes a deep breath and exhales:*

Zara   . . . can y'believe it? shaadi outfits . . .

Yasmin *picks up the newspaper. A beat as she considers:*

Yasmin (*wry*)   . . . we could get something ready-made off
the peg . . . Bombay Stores . . .

Zara *shakes her head, dismissing this idea.*

Yasmin   like we used to . . . eat at Mumtaz's, get a drive-
thru McFlurry on the way home, be like old times . . . won't
it?

Zara   thanks, but got too much on . . .

Yasmin   could go tomorrow, if you're busy today, I've taken
the week off – do whatever you need me to do . . .

Zara   a week!?!

Yasmin   yeah – just jump in me car . . .

Zara   spent enough monies on the fabric, got the shoes, matching indigo jewellery, silver bag . . . don't you worry, Yas, we're alright, I'll get it all sorted . . .

Yasmin (*looking around*)   looks like it . . .

Yasmin *considers the newspaper again:*

y'sleeping alright? I haven't slept properly since /

Zara   did y'come snakes pass then? shouldn't risk it should ya snakes pass if the weather's not [good]

Yasmin (*shows* **Zara** *the can of Red Bull*)   weather's not too bad / thankfully.

Zara   we can keep an eye on it, the weather, depending on how long you wanna, y'know, stay – juss thinking shouldn't risk it, when it rains should yer? mashallah . . . hasn't rained today . . . that's something . . . Allah Tallah looking out for you.

Yasmin (*still holding the newspaper*)   just got here . . . d'ya want me to go then? look /

Zara (*texting*)   no, no! course not . . . just let me try Khalda again . . . see if she'll . . . just . . . y'know . . . then I'll get us . . . [a drink] . . . wasn't expecting yer was I? wasn't expecting yer to just walk in after two years. I mean of all the times, Yas – why / now?

Yasmin *unfolds the newspaper with 'The Grooming Gang Reign of Terror' headline and the mugshots of the gang:*

Yasmin   our Raheel . . .

Points to one of the pictures of a gallery of men in the headline:

in this line up!!!

Zara *glares at* **Yasmin** . . .

Yasmin   what's going on, Zara?

Zara *continues to glare at* **Yasmin** *in disbelief, disgusted at the 'accusation'.* **Zara** *grabs the newspaper:*

Zara   you bringin' that into my home!!!

Yasmin   !

Zara *grabs the newspaper and frantically rips it up.*

Yasmin   !

Zara   do not bring this shit into my home – ever!

Zara *shoves the newspaper in the bin.* **Zara**'*s asthma is triggered. She searches for her inhaler, finds it, she inhales, angry at the accusation:*

Zara   ever!

Zara *inhales her inhaler again.* **Yasmin** *observes* **Zara**'*s struggle with her asthma:*

Yasmin   no one's answering our calls.

Beat.

Jamal and me, reading *that* on our own . . .

Zara   you're a piece of work . . .

(*Laughs to herself, slightly hysterical:*) I got to finish these, I've got the khatham tonight, trip to do tomorrow, for work, wedding outfits to sort now as well. . .

Beat.

Yasmin   what is going on, Zara?

Beat.

Zara   . . . and you wonder why I don't call you back . . . looking at me like that, that look that the goras give us . . . do you really believe Raheel would have anything to do with this?

Beat.

my own flesh n blood, do you know me at all? my sister, does she even know me!? *my* sister . . . they arrested him. they arrested loads of us they came for my son. but they've nothing. they've got nothing on him. he's innocent. how the fff' how the . . . y'know those rags hate us. where you been living, under a rock, Yasmin!!?

Beat.

Yasmin   I know, Zara! I know what they do. I know that . . . and . . . I know you *my* sister . . . I know. it's just that . . . it's just . . . [no one gets in touch with us]

Zara   we're gonna sue the arses off them . . . don't worry about that . . . we're gonna rinse them.

Yasmin   who's supporting you? here. now.

Zara   the onions . . . they're expecting them . . . the khatham, I said.

Zara *carries on but can't really slice the onions despite best efforts.*

Yasmin   just leave the fucking onions will ya!

Beat.

for fuck's sake – let me – move over.

Yasmin *takes over the peeling and slicing – silenced – noticing the knife is blunt, she sharpens the knife; slightly confused as to where things are as* **Zara** *has redecorated the kitchen since the last time she was here:*

Zara   ?

Yasmin   who's supporting you? who's been round to see you, to help you?

Zara   a couple of people . . .

Yasmin   who?

Zara   . . .

Yasmin   who, Zara?

Zara   Zahir

Yasmin   Zahir, the prat!!

Zara   he's got friends . . . he's helping me.

Yasmin   but . . . Zahir!

Zara   don't start, Yasmin . . . DON'T. NEED. IT!

Pause.

if y'wanna help? check the pizza will ya. in the oven?

Beat.

Yasmin *goes to check.*

Yasmin   not ready . . .

She returns to slicing:

Beat.

here, I'm slicing, don't even know who's died.

Zara   Nasreen's mum aunty, she calls her Beyji.

Yasmin   you ever meet her?

Zara   not the point.

everyone's doing their bit, like usual, cos we stick together.

Yasmin   . . .

Yasmin   yeah, everyone's a brother, a sister, an aunty an uncle, all one ummah ey? unless you're different, don't matter if you're a hypocrite like Zahir, does it?

Zara   even the / goras [help each other out at funerals and that].

Yasmin   does it?

Zara   we're about 'we are', Yasmin, not the western notion of 'I am'.

Yasmin   . . . be great if the 'we' wasn't so selective ey?

Zara   let me tell you this, people know me round here, known me from time, all the work I've done growing 'centre' . . . I've got respect round here, goras, Polish, Kalas, Romanians, everyone!

only thing that's kept me going, everyone knowing me, knowing that I. know. my. son.

Beat.

Yasmin   where is he? Raheel?

Zara   . . .

Yasmin   where's he working?

Zara   . . .

Yasmin   ?

Zara   Zahir's shop.

Yasmin (*stops peeling*)   fuckinell, Zara!

Zara   'least Zahir doesn't believe everything he reads in those dirty rags . . . ey?! donates direct debit to my centre . . . all the flippin' cuts we've had to deal with . . . don't know where we'd be without him . . .

Yasmin   no skin off his nose, inheriting *our* dad's business is it?

Zara   his dad's business as well – thaya's.

Yasmin   our dad's as well . . .

Beat.

Zara (*referring to the finished peeled, sliced onions and garlic*) right.

thanks. can you cover them?

Points to where the cling film is: In the bottom cupboard. **Yasmin**
*goes to collect the cling film – still struggling to navigate this new
kitchen.*

Zara   not sure I can drive with this (*referring to her cut finger*).

Yasmin *covers the onions:*

Yasmin   got my car . . .

Zara   thanks. I can get a lift . . . I'll just drop a text.

Zara *striving and failing to text with her cut finger.* **Yasmin**
observes this:

Yasmin   I said . . . I can help . . . Zara . . .?

Zara   they'll come get me, khatham isn't far . . .

Yasmin   but I'm here, already.

Zara   why don't ya rest, ey?

Yasmin   rest!!?

Zara   would ya mind checking the pizza again . . .

and while you're there get kettle on . . .

got these herbal teas – peppermint, honey and lemon,
mango and pineapple with ginseng . . . I love that one? fancy
one?

Yasmin *shakes her head.*

or do you want builder's?

Yasmin *checks the pizza. It's ready. She gets it out onto the side.*

Zara   juss can't help peeing myself, if I drink builder's tea,
can't risk it, these herbal teas, they don't make you wee as
much do they? they should put that on adverts shouldn't
they? 'herbal tea, doesn't make you wee' I'm a poet and I
know it! so pick one – relax!!

Yasmin   your *purrka* no one's gonna notice if you pee
yourself in that . . .

Zara   all about the '*ber-ka*' is it, Yasmin?

Yasmin   said '*purrrka*' – not '*ber-ka*' dint I . . .
I'm not a fucking gora!

Yasmin *pointedly now puts the cooked pizza in front of* **Zara**.

Zara (*looking at her phone*)   why's no one answering?
Sofe'll drive me with these [onions].

Yasmin   Sofe's driving!?

Zara   yeah, I wouldn't have passed her . . .

Yasmin *starts to cut the pizza:*

Zara   knocked a wing mirror off someone's car the other
day . . . it's good it isn't far ey?

Yasmin   grow up too fast don't they.

Zara   Jamal, what's he up to then?

Yasmin   dropped out of uni.

Zara   no!

Yasmin   s'alright. for the best. in the end.

Zara   haven't seen him since he was applying. dropped out?

Yasmin   but you know what, Zara / . . .

Zara   oh, Yas, dropped out of uni . . . y'Allah!

Beat.

Yasmin   he's a manager at Oasis . . .

Zara   manager? at Oasis?!

Yasmin   yeah.

Zara   oh I love Oasis, I do.

Beat.

the kids, all doing well aren't they? manager at Oasis, working, studying . . .

Yasmin   but this weekend . . . it's like . . . he just moved out and in with / . . .

Zara   big now ey? can't keep them little forever, can we?

Yasmin   I know . . .

Zara   kids'd love to see him.

Yasmin (*exasperated*)   here, pizza!

Both sisters sit to eat.

Awkward pause.

Yasmin   when did you last eat? look at ya . . .

Zara (*shrugs*)   got salad in the fridge.

Yasmin *gets the salad, piles it on the plates.*

Yasmin   come on . . . eat . . .

Beat.

how's she taken all this, Sofe?

Zara   d'y'know what, *I am* worried about her, sits upstairs on her own, on social media . . . drives me up the wall . . . calls herself 'the purple hijab'.

Yasmin   ?

Zara   at. the. purple. hijab . . . on this twitter.

Yasmin   purple hijab?

Zara   nine-eleven generation ennit, Yas . . .

Sudden loud banging on the front door – offstage.

Yasmin, *startled.* **Zara** *doesn't flinch.*

Zara *deliberately carries on as per normal:*

Yasmin   you not going to see who it is?

Zara   I know who it is . . .

Yasmin   ???

Encourages **Yasmin** *to check.* **Yasmin** *sits – puzzled, nervous . . .*

Zara   think *you* should check for me.

Yasmin   ???

Zara   go on then please . . . baji . . .

Yasmin *cautiously exits.*

Yasmin (*offstage*)   uuuugh. bastards!

Yasmin *returns. She is holding 'the' newspaper article –* *'Grooming Gang Reign of Terror' headline smeared with dogshit.*

Yasmin   !!!

Zara *nonchalantly hands* **Yasmin** *a carrier bag:*

Zara   put it in that plastic bag. roll up that newspaper left on the floor – that's what it's there for . . .

She hands another old newspaper to **Yasmin**.

Zara   here put this down after . . .

Yasmin, *stunned, takes the stuff and exits to the front.*

Zara *carries on as per normal – cleaning, sorting – deadpan.*

Yasmin, *disgusted, returns with the dirty article and everything else in the carrier bag.*

Zara   throw it out the back. . .

Yasmin   fuckinell, Zara!

Zara *sprays the air with air freshener like clockwork.* **Yasmin** *goes out the back door to the bins.*

Zara *deadpan clears the pizza stuff.*

Yasmin *returns.* **Zara** *hands the cleaning stuff to* **Yasmin** *like clockwork.* **Yasmin** *speechless.*

Yasmin *goes back to the front [offstage] to clean the floor:*

Zara   tuesday – day after they put *your* nephew in the paper, it happened three times . . . used up two bottles of Flash scrubbing till my hands were sore . . . twice the next day, then nowt till now . . . must've known you were coming, ey?

Yasmin *returns. Shocked.*

Zara *carries on as per normal.*

Yasmin *throws the dirty tissues out the bins in the back via the back door. She returns.*

Yasmin *washes her hands – stunned. She then gets her key and intentionally locks the back door then leans her back to the door and breathes – slightly out of breath.*

Zara *is still nonchalant.*

Zara   . . .

Yasmin   . . .

Zara   wednesday . . . Raheel nearly got attacked, decides he wants to go out Yas, I tells him not to, as a mum y'know don't ya? but he was like 'I ant done anything amma, no one's gonna believe it.'

only made it to the bus stop; them haramzade, Britain's First, spotted him, managed to outrun them . . . but it's knocked him Yas . . . wouldn't speak . . . till Zahir came over that night . . . got through to him. thank God for Zahir – I'm not joking – he's took him under his wing, give him a job in the shop there and then. somewhere he's safe . . . alhamdulillah.

Long pause as **Yasmin** *absorbs everything.*

Yasmin   . . .

Zara   . . .

Yasmin   could have come to me, couldn't he tho? Raheel, stay with me and Jamal couldn't he?

Zara   oh he's fine, he's settled in now . . .

Beat

Yasmin   we're 'own', aren't we? get the boys together again . . . they'll be looking for Christmas staff at Jamal's . . . could get him some Christmas work / Jamal could . . .

Zara   thanks, he's settled / Yasmin, insha'Allah.

Yasmin   just a temporary job . . . keep him busy . . . away from here.

Zara   if you do your duas, your duties . . . everything will work out, won't it. . .

Yasmin   but those thugs if they get him /

Zara   he's growing a beard, we've changed his hair, keeps his hat on, he's with his uncle all day, he's alright . . .

Yasmin   [sounds it!]

Zara   feel like I'm worrying you Yas, but it's gonna be okay. we're okay.

Yasmin   . . .

Zara *manages to text Nasreen that the onions are ready, now that her hand is a bit better.*

Yasmin   Zahir though?

Zara   just let it go, Yasmin . . . move on, will ya!

Yasmin   . . .

Zara   he's changed . . . he really has, he's different now . . .

Yasmin   bet he's not.

Zara   what about you, Yas . . . getting mashed up by the rec singing really loud thinking you're Kylie Minogue / off your head

Yasmin   Kylie!?

Zara ending up rat-arsed like a besharam, banging your head then ending up in hospital . . . poor abba having to come to collect you, I mean, the shame of it!

Yasmin cos you grassed me up, Zara!

Zara they wanted a parent – couldn't contact mum could I?! no one, not one person said a word to you . . . you got off lightly there . . .

Yasmin I dint tho, did I? Zahir just threw me under the bus, he gets away with his road-man ways, no one scrutinises him in the way they do me . . . us . . . do they? spied on, reported on

Beat.

he gets away with it all!

Zara and look at us now, big grown women, grown-up children, doing really well . . . who would've thought we'd ever get our shit together . . . me n you, couple of twits . . .

Beat.

Yasmin all he has to do is show up at jummah, put on a robe / and the

Zara n what's wrong with that . . .? n what is wrong with that? turning up at mosque in a robe?? what is wrong with that, Yasmin!? internalised islamophobia is not a good look y'know . . .

Yasmin and what about internalised misogyny, ey?

Beat.

no one bats an eyelid when married men have a string of kids scattered round town. that's. what's. wrong. with. that. Zara!

Zara everyone's moved on, why can't you? he's grown-up, he has, all that matters is my son's safe, please, Yas.

Yasmin . . .

Zara   still a drama queen aren't ya . . .!

Sofia *enters from the back door, has a hijab on and earphones:*

Sofia   khala!! [*aunt*] is it you?

Takes off her earphones and headscarf.

Yasmin   Sofia!

look at you . . . all grown!

Sofia   it's good you've come, khala!

Yasmin *gives* **Sofia** *a big hug.* **Sofia** *notices* **Zara**'s *hand.*

Sofia   you alright, amma?

Zara   just a little cut, am okay . . . silly accident.

Sofia   when did you get here, khala?

Yasmin   not long, just got here really . . .

Sofia   Jamal here?

Yasmin   no, he's, err, working . . .

Sofia   you come for the demo?

Yasmin   what demo . . .?

Sofia   khala . . . you don't know . . .?

Zara *shakes her head . . .* **Sofia** *tears up.*

Sofia   you don't know khala . . .?

Yasmin   know what?

Sofia   khala . . . this old Yemini man . . . last tuesday he got kicked to death coming home from fajr, called him a groomer . . .

Yasmin   what!

Zara   that dint make the front pages did it!?

Yasmin   kicked to death coming home from fajr!?

Sofia *and* **Zara** *nod.*

Zara (*prayer*)   Inna lillahi wa inna ilayhi raji'un

Pause.

Sofia   they're all by that bed-shop, mum, these big fat goras with their union jacks, n these big red cross flags . . . it's scary, really scary, mum.

Yasmin   EDL?

Sofia   you wouldn't believe it, amma, someone had this banner saying 'Mohammad sallallahu-wasallam, is' . . . I can't even say it – nearly made me sick . . . and, I saw Mrs Newman from school there . . .

Zara   your uncle said dint he? the goras they've got it in for us . . .

Yasmin   why haven't they reported this!

Zara   as if they're going to report that, Yas . . . us going about our day to day, then getting murdered for going about our day to day.

Yasmin   . . . should've called me, Zara!

Zara   wouldn't change anything, would it?

Yasmin   how can they not report an innocent murdered man?

Beat.

Zara   why you shocked, Yas? you forgotten what it's like? that time you got pushed in the water down Milltown Baths and no one came to help us, nearly drowned – you!

Yasmin   I thought we'd moved on.

Zara   not anymore, not round here.

Sofia   it's really bad round here, khala.

Zara (*to* **Sofia**)   where's Raheel?

Sofia   looking after the shop.

Zara   good . . .

(*To* **Yasmin**.) EDL, Britain First and all the other goons, they've been up here all week.

Sofia   it's not safe . . .

Zara   don't hear of that anywhere do you.

Yasmin   . . .

Sofia   we've got our very first counter demo, khala. new people tho, friends of uncle, they've come, these brothers, apne, driven all the way down to be on our side, it's really good, amma, it really is: 'New Dawn' we're gonna call ourselves, iss good innit . . . all them apne come all this way to support us, I mean . . .

Zara   alhamdulillah . . .

Yasmin (*to* **Zara**)   shouldn't we go then? this counter demo?

Zara   no, let them sort it . . .

Yasmin   Zara?

Sofia   uncle said I'm best going home cos there'll be trouble.

Yasmin   !

Zara   wouldn't make any difference, us there or not, would it?

Yasmin   of course it would . . . makes all the difference . . . we've got to do something.

Zara *starts texting the replacement dressmaker for shaadi outfits.*

Yasmin   how many demos we used to be on back in the day, Zara?

Zara   got other priorities now, Yas . . .

(*To* **Sofia**.) is it churidar you want, Sofe, for your indigo suit?

Sofia   ?

Zara   the wedding? churidar or just salwar for your indigo one? for sunday? c'mon, what is it you want?

Sofia   oh errr, churidar, mum . . . churidar is fine, mum . . .

Yasmin   wedding outfits!?

Zara   this new dressmaker . . . she needs the work, Khalda said, insha'Allah she can do it . . .

Yasmin   Zara!?

Zara   it's a wedding.

life goes on, Yas.

Yasmin   what's happened to you?

Zara   it's all in hand, Yas . . . that's all.

Sofia   yes, khala, brothers have come.

Zara   let the brothers get on with it.

Sofia's *phone pings, she checks:*

Sofia   they're going now, the brothers are gathering . . .

Yasmin   what's all this 'brothers'?

Sofia   uncle and New Dawn, everyone, it's well sik, khala . . .

Yasmin   any sisters?

Sofia   *still checking her messages* and some gorey, 'the anti-Nazi league', they're there.

Zara   alhamdulillah . . .

Sofia   gonna be their 'social media strategist', we were chatting about it just before I came home.

Zara   ?

Sofia   good isn't it, mum! 'social. media. strategist' use my skillz proper . . .

Yasmin   old men murdered coming home from fajr, an innocent young man falsely accused and chased, dog shit getting posted through letter boxes . . . and we're at home chopping onions, peeling thom, planning bloomin' wedding outfits!

Sofia   already set up a twitter handle . . . 36 followers and growing . . .

Yasmin   let's go!

Zara *packed and ready to take the onions and stuff to the khatham.*

Zara   it's a khatham, Yasmin . . .

(*To* **Sofia**.) once we've dropped these off you can get on with that project, don't think I've forgotten . . . that drop in your grade.

Sofia   mum! it's just the idiot tutor innit chattin' I told ya, I'll make that up . . . it's just one little slip, that's all! / serious!

Zara (*to* **Yasmin**)   make yourself a drink, Yas, we won't be long . . .

Zara *putting her headscarf and coat on.* **Zara** *passes* **Sofia** *her coat and headscarf.*

Yasmin   Zara!?

Zara   just got to drop these off that's all . . .

Yasmin   so let's just drop it off . . . go to the demo – hour round trip – sorted!

Zara *and* **Sofia**, *ready to step out of the back door.*

Yasmin   think about it . . . this . . . this . . . Nasreen's mum's beyji, whoever she is, she's probably looking down from the very vantage point she's got now screaming 'get the fuck out there'!!

Sofia *gasps!!!*

Zara   Yasmin!

Sofia (*to* **Yasmin** *impressed by her aunt*)   I wanted to go, khala
. . .

Zara *shoves her and* **Sofia** *out of the back door.*

Zara   back in five!

The door slams shut.

Beat.

Yasmin   and your uncle told you to go home, did he?

She sighs. Sits. Rests over the table with her head on her arms. Exasperated by everything.

She looks at her phone.

She scrolls her contacts, puts it on speaker and dials.

The phone rings and rings. Cuts the call.

Redials the phone. Rings and rings. Cuts the call.

Redials – phone goes to voicemail: 'hiya, it's Jamal. leave a message and I'll get back to ya . . .'

Yasmin   Jamal, just me, call me back will ya? I'm in Forestdale, really need to speak with you . . . got loads to fill you in on . . . get in touch, will ya?

Beat.

I hope you're *both* okay?

call me . . .

There is a sudden loud knock on the front door. The same voice from the start:

Voice   Aunty Zara, is that you . . .?

Yasmin *cuts her call.*

Yasmin   ?

Voice   Aunty Zara?

Aunty Zara   . . . anyone in? Raheel, Sofia? anyone in?

Knocking continues as **Yasmin** *walks to the front door – offstage. She opens the door.*

Yasmin (*offstage*)   hello

Voice   hi! Aunty Zara, Raheel, they in?

Yasmin   no, no one's in / can I

Voice   no one's in?

still!?

Yasmin   no, they've just nipped out / can I help at all . . .

Voice   are you sure no one's in?

Yasmin   no, they've just nipped out . . . I'm Zara's sister, Yasmin / if you want / [to leave a message]

Jade   Yasmin!

Yasmin! Jamal's mum, you've come!

Yasmin   !

errr come in.

Jade   how is he, Jamal?

Beat.

Yasmin   he's okay, he's, and you are . . .?

Jade   Jade . . . Jade Steel.

Beat.

Yasmin   Jade!

Beat.

Steel!

Jade   yeah.

see me on the news?

Yasmin   the paper . . . I saw you / in *The Chronicle*.

Jade   yeah.

I complained, I did, they've put an apology in today . . . have you seen it? page 8, have you seen it?

Yasmin   !

Jade   has Aunty Zara and Raheel – has everyone seen it – the apology?!

Yasmin *shakes her head.*

Jade   they've got to see it
he would never . . . he would never . . .
I swear down I went ballistic.

whoa . . . she's changed it . . . all the units
looks nice, better,
that prick did a shit job anyway
don't blame her for changing it.

Yasmin   . . .

Jade   where is she . . .? Aunty Zara? Raheel?

Yasmin   just nipped round the corner, shouldn't be too long . . .

Jade   I keep trying – yesterday, day before that . . . I keep trying . . . she's not answering . . . the door I think . . .

Yasmin   she's err, she's not answering the door to you?

Jade   think I know why
turned me against her dint he . . .

Beat.

when I was here, that Sajid . . .

Yasmin   Sajid?

Jade   Sajid Baig.

Yasmin   ???

Jade   said she's not proper in her deen, that none of 'em really care about me . . . using me to keep her funding at the women's centre, that's what he said . . . imagine how that made me feel? I told her to get lost and eff off, was proper raging . . . feel bad now, all a pack of lies, it's my therapist who keeps telling me 'it's not my fault' what he fukin' did? sorry . . .

Beat.

I'd love to see Raheel . . . all of them – speak with them . . .

(*Whispers.*) it was juss Sajid, brainwashing me!

Yasmin   slow down. who's this Sajid?

Jade   y'know – Sajid Baig – ringleader!
oh oh – shit – y'don't know do ya? she hasn't told yer, has she?

Yasmin   you met this Sajid, ringleader, here?

Jade   . . .

Jade (*quiet*)   Sajid Baig. decorator. that's how it started.

Jade *looking around.*

shit – I'm so sorry. thought you knew. thought everyone knew.

look, is Raheel definitely not in?

Yasmin   at work . . .

Jade   he's not at the call centre. I tried there. they said he's left . . .

Yasmin   works in a shop now.

Jade   uncle Zahir's shop?

Yasmin   you know uncle Zahir?

Jade (*nods*)   dint think he liked him – Raheel.

Yasmin   he tell you that?

Jade   we were like 'that' . . . used to be . . .

Crosses her fingers to indicate their closeness:

I heard about you n all, he liked you . . . and Jamal . . . a lot.

Yasmin   . . .

Jade   it's just you liked a drink, dint ya? got pregnant to a rasta n had to leave the area.

bhesti . . .

Beat.

Yasmin   I wouldn't put it like that.

Jade   it's okay, no one cares [about girls] not round 'ere . . . look at me, police never even took a statement, just kept telling me to behave myself.

Beat.

Yasmin   how long is it . . . you've, you've known . . . everyone?

Jade   since year 7:

Aunty Zara she helped me mum fill in the free school meals forms, down at the centre . . . my mum weren't well then Raheel fed me – gave me stuff from his own dinners. gave me all sorts. that's why it's wrong what they've done to Raheel?!

Yasmin   !

Jade   that fucking journalist – driven all the way from London to 'listen to our stories' in a bougie teashop, nob. all I tells him is I met Sajid here . . . I gave him all 'our stories' like about nice uncle Ahmed, he got me away from 'em all, and he had cancer when he did that; Raheel giving me food . . . we tell 'em this stuff, but they don't listen to that bit, Aunty Zara and Raheel helping me and me mum, and now my new life with Ishmail, that's my husband – he's a Muslim – and my little boy, Jaden . . .

. . . why dint he print that!?

Beat.

Yasmin   what was Zara, why, would she . . . what . . .?

Jade   we weren't the only one taken in by Sajid and his lot, me n Aunty Zara . . . everyone was . . . if it wasn't me, it'd been some other girl somewhere else . . . that's what really gets me, everyone wanting to go on about us being vulnerable, well, what I wanna say is how you're all gullible, lazy or friggin' stupid, or don't even care . . . he groomed me . . . he groomed 'everyone', before he did anything . . . that's what gets me mad . . . 'poor girls groomed by these men', I just wanna say 'nah! you were all groomed, all of ya!'

Beat.

Yasmin   she had *him* here in this house?

Jade   will she be back soon? my babysitter's on the clock.

Yasmin   she's only nipped round the corner.

Jade   traffic's bad tho, with the EDL and everything, my bus got rerouted again earlier . . . taking like forever . . .

Beat.

cos thing is – I been offered a book deal for 'my story' . . . and this book . . . I wanna write it with her – cos with everything that's going on I wanna help her and Raheel, she can give her side n all, can't she? could use a pseudonym if she wants the girls who no one talks about. just think: Aunty Zara and Jade Steel's book . . . cos I was thirteen, but there was this other girl, and she was from primary school and . . . and . . . and . . . and . . . she's missing . . . (*Deep exhale.*) never mind . . .

Yasmin   !

Jade's *alarm on her phone pings.* **Jade** *looks.*

Jade (*stands*)   my Jaden . . . babysitter . . . he's only six months . . .

you will tell her all this won't you . . . I'll come back later –
cos I'm meeting this publisher tomorrow – but give her this
. . .

Jade *offers* **Yasmin** *a scrap piece of paper with her number written on it.*

tell her to call me . . .
you will won't ya?

Yasmin (*stands, takes the slip of paper*)   yeah, yeah, I will,
yeah . . .

Jade   you will give it her and Raheel, won't ya'?

Yasmin   yeah, course I will . . .

As they exit to the front – offstage.

Jade (*offstage*)   I'll try and come back though – I'll try.

Yasmin   I'll tell 'em . . . I will . . .

Jade *exits.*

Yasmin *returns frazzled, thinks, scrambles to find her phone:*

Yasmin   fuck!

As **Yasmin** *dials,* **Zara**'s *phone rings out on the side – where she had left it.*

Yasmin   shit!

She picks up **Zara**'s *phone and starts to scroll to see if she can see 'Sajid' in the contacts.*

Raheel *enters behind her – doesn't immediately recognise the woman in the kitchen and cautiously approaches, which disturbs her:*

Yasmin   Raheel!! /

Raheel   khala! it's you . . .!

Yasmin   you gave me the fright of my life!

She goes to her nephew and hugs him. Then gives him another tighter hug as if she's so worried about her nephew.

look at you! all big, grown just like Jamal . . .

Raheel where's mum?

Yasmin nipped to drop some stuff off for the khatham.

She hugs him tight again. **Raheel** *finally breaks free.*

Raheel Jamal, he, not here?

Yasmin *shakes her head.*

Raheel hasn't been from time . . .

Yasmin just busy today working n that . . .

Awkward pause as **Yasmin**'*s eyes follow* **Raheel** *as he gets a plate, a slice of pizza, a bit of salad.* **Yasmin** *nods then watches him exit upstairs.*

Zara *and* **Sofia** *burst in through the door:*

Zara but he said, your tutor / it's a significant drop!

Sofia just half an hour, mum, please?

Zara how many more times, Sofia!

Sofia we've got this massive crowd, khala . . . 'bout time we stood up for ourselves int it!

(*To* **Zara**.) if we stay at the side it'll be alright won't it, mum?

Zara *ignores* **Sofia**.

Yasmin (*wryly*) in Islam, the Prophet's wives Khadeejah, Aisha they never stayed on the side, they led, dint they, Zara?

Zara well, we're not in the Arabian desert now you know, Yasmin.

Zara *hands* **Yasmin** *the washing-up liquid to wash the empty bowls she's returned with.* **Yasmin** *puts it down.*

Zara (*to* **Sofia**) homework . . .

Sofia   but, mum! you and khala you'd go on loads of demos, you said dint ya when you were my age . . . khala said . . . dint ya, khala?

Yasmin *nods.*

Zara   for your nani's sake, Sofia, think about it . . .!

Yasmin   yeah, Sofia, can't have the Sharif daughters on the streets, scrapping, fighting with the men . . . y'know, cos that would be the kanjeree, the divorcee, the whores of Babylon, haram police'll be on fire! got to keep up appearances ey, Zara?

Sofia (*under her breath*)   truedat!

Zara (*perplexed*)   for the good of the family, [and my centre] can't you stand with me on this, her grade has dropped! whose side you on, Yas?

Yasmin   whose side you on, Zara?

Beat.

Zara (*perplexed*)   what!?

Sofia   what's the point in going to a uni full of drunk people, anyway?

Zara   there aren't just drunk people at uni, Sofia: Ryan's going, he isn't a drunk, Iram's going she isn't a drunk, Shaheen's going she isn't a drunk.

Yasmin   believe me, Sofia, being drunk doesn't discriminate . . . I can vouch for that.

Zara   Yasmin!

Yasmin *backs off.* **Sofia** *reluctantly gets her homework out of her bag, and her tech. She checks her phone:*

Sofia   whoa! up to 63 followers!

Beat.

not sure I'm bothered about uni, mum.

Zara   not again . . .

Sofia   I been reading online.

Zara   not again!

Sofia   this one man, black man, stopped and searched when he walked into a university . . .

Zara   how many more times, Sofia . . . if you look for it you'll find it . . .

Sofia   the security stopped, searched him, patted him down

Zara   please . . . get offline . . . please focus on your coursework / please . . .

Sofia   n y'know what, mum . . . y'know what, mum . . . he was a lecturer! a lecturer!

Beat.

gap year, amma? help? with New Dawn or with you? marketing person or something – down the centre?

Zara   what do you know about marketing?

Sofia   learn on the job couldn't I? like you do, mum . . .

Zara   you'll throw away your education because of all of this.

Sofia   it's only a gap year, amma! seriously, that is it!

I mean you never went to uni did you, mum, n look at you?

Zara   I'm tired of repeating myself, Sofia, we don't let this nastiness, stop us . . . it's a khatham later, we've got a shaadi to sort, you have your revision – this bakwaas has nothing to do with us, is. not. our. making!

Sofia   I know, mum, but that's not what I'm saying . . .

Zara   you still need to get a place, even if it's a gap year . . . otherwise it's just, just, another year . . .

Sofia   isn't if I reapply.

Raheel *enters with an empty plate having eaten the pizza.*

Beat.

Zara (*looking at* **Yasmin**)   [why didn't you tell us] didn't know you were in!

Yasmin *shrugs.* **Sofia** *absorbed in checking her online activity.*

Zara   you're early?

Raheel *shrugs.*

Zara   you eaten?

Raheel *shrugs.*

Zara   uncle, he's not fed you?

Raheel   just had / . . .

Zara   you want some more pizza?

I've got dahl in the fridge if you want?

Zara *picks the takeaway leaflets from earlier, and shows them to* **Raheel***:*

shall I pick you a takeaway? here . . . sit down . . .

Raheel *shakes his head in exasperation:*

Zara   khala's here, come and sit . . .

Raheel *feels he has to sit.*

Zara *sorts some more pizza and salad for her children. She offers them their plates:*

Sofia   . . . not your fancy-pants pizza again mum, I had a Subway . . .

Zara (*pleased*)   with Iram, Saira n Shaheen?

Sofia   no, New Dawn before the demo . . . God! this is so [infuriating] I know Raheel can't go, but we should . . .

Raheel (*to* **Sofia**)   uncle told us both of us to come home, to stay out of it, so that's what we do . . . listen to him, alright!

Awkward silence. **Zara** *pours everyone some nimbu-pani whilst* **Raheel** *eats.*

She then looks for her mobile that she had left earlier. Finds it, sees that **Yasmin** *called.*

Zara   Yas, you call me when we were out?

Yasmin   yes, because you had a visitor:

Yasmin *passes the paper with* **Jade**'s *number on it to* **Zara**.

Jade Steel.

Zara   !

Sofia   !

Yasmin   !

Raheel   course she came round, because this is where she met him dint she!? mum kept letting him eat with us, stay with us, a few times . . .

He gets up and leaves.

Zara   Raheel!

Zara *looks at* **Yasmin**. [what does she know?]

Sofia   mum . . . it's okay. it's okay, mum. mum, you okay?

Zara   Yasmin . . . I . . .

Sofia   don't worry, mum, it's gonna be okay, mum . . .

Zara   he was a decorator, needed the work / and I

Sofia   it's okay, mum . . . listen . . .

Yasmin   Zara, what the . . .

Zara's *and* **Sofia**'s *phones start buzzing.*

Zara *looks at* **Yasmin**. **Yasmin** *holds it.*

*Zara's and **Sofia***'s *phones continue to frantically buzz.* **Zara** *and* **Yasmin** *keep looking at each other.*

Sofia *checks her phone.*

Zara   . . .

Yasmin   . . .

Sofia   mum! they've arrested our men!

mum, khala, they've arrested our men, mum! mum!

Zara (*coming to her senses*! *checks her phone*)   where?

Sofia   arrested them outside the Admiral Arms, they'd been kettled . . .

She shows her khala her phone/tech:

Yasmin   Admiral Arms, that old BNP pub?

Sofia   they've got Iqbal brothers, Mo, Fiaz, Aftab, Mohammad, Iftikar, others – shit! taking them to the police station . . . mum! mum!

Zara *checks her phone.*

Yasmin   quick!

Zara   got to get down there, quick, make noise . . .

Sofia *and* **Zara** *grab their coats and headscarves:*

Sofia (*ready to go*)   c'mon, mum . . .

Zara (*looks at* **Yasmin**)   you not coming?

Yasmin   I'll stay with Raheel. make sure he stays here . . .

Zara   . . .

Yasmin   go on, we'll be fine . . . someone's got to keep an eye on him . . .

Zara *reluctantly agrees, nodding.* **Zara** *and* **Sofia** *exit.*

Raheel *comes downstairs with his phone.*

Raheel   can you believe this, khala?!

Yasmin   sadly, I can . . .

Raheel (*looking around*)   they gone? they gone to the police station?

Yasmin *nods.*

Raheel   I should go . . . I need to be there!

Yasmin   no Raheel, stay out of it! your uncle's right on this one. okay . . .?

okay?

She pulls a chair for **Raheel** *to sit. He sits.*

Raheel   they won't leave us alone! y'know they kicked that innocent man to death, they were calling him a dirty groomer . . . the police gave my picture to the paper, could be me next, couldn't it!?

Beat.

Yasmin   I know, Raheel, I know / but you are safe, we're all here.

Raheel   we're gonna sue them y'know that! we're gonna sue them . . .

He expresses frustration, bangs his fists on the table.

Yasmin *attempts to lighten the mood, and starts to make* **Raheel** *a mug of tea.*

Yasmin   c'mon . . . here, let me make you drink? what do you want?

your mum's got a bit of a collection here . . .

Raheel *shrugs . . .* **Yasmin** *just continues to make her nephew a drink.*

Raheel *rubs his arms, which ache.*

Yasmin   you still have one sugar?

Raheel *nods.*

Yasmin   what do you do day to day? keeping busy, ey? tell your aunty . . .

Raheel   shift the veg n stuff, take the deliveries . . . might go to the warehouse next week . . .

Yasmin   well, if it's got to be done . . . best to keep busy isn't it? as your mum says . . . like Dory, just keep swimming, swimming, swimming . . . I bloomin' get what she means now!

Raheel   *mum!* you didn't know did yer?

Yasmin   so much I don't know . . .

Beat.

does she know anyone else in that line up? do you?

Raheel   no – already been over a million times with uncle. just Sajid, that's all! n I only met him cos of her, dint I? uncle said he'd warned her – to stick with her own brothers and sisters – too relaxed with people wasn't she?

Yasmin   here's yer tea.

Pause.

wait! what? what does uncle mean, 'too relaxed with people'?

Raheel   juss helping anyone and everyone, even let that paedo in here!

Yasmin   to help him?

Raheel   needed some work – like she said, decorator.

Yasmin   ?

Yasmin   *just* a decorator?

Raheel   not even a good one – she's too quick to help people!

Slight pause as **Yasmin** *considers:*

Yasmin   how do we know if we're helping good people or bad? isn't it our deen to help others, Raheel? like Jade, this Jade, she said something about you helping her. fed her or something. she told some journalist you helped her, when she needed it most . . .

Beat.

Raheel   does Jamal think I did it then?

Yasmin   no.

Raheel   he does, doesn't he?

Yasmin   no! course not!

Raheel   cos why didn't he come today?

Yasmin   . . .

Raheel   I think he does suspect, doesn't he? is that why you came, to find out if your nephew was, what, a groomer?

Yasmin   we know you'd never, Raheel.

Raheel   so why's he unfriend me then? Facebook . . .

Yasmin   he's blocking me too, Raheel. *my* calls.

Raheel   he should come back here.

Yasmin   he has his own life now . . .

Raheel   we used to be like brothers. close. came every summer. shared my room, every summer. then he just stopped coming dint he?

Yasmin   just grew up that's all . . .

Raheel   uncle Zahir says if you want to get anywhere in this life, you best stick with the people you trust. uncle Zahir says that.

Yasmin   . . .

Raheel   people come all over to Zahir's! – his shop, he built with his bare hands.

Yasmin   well everyone needs their fruit and veg.

Raheel   tell him come work with us, we could use someone like him. uncle was saying that would be for the best. he'll be good . . . and you come back here too, just need to look the part . . . cover up n that, you'll be alright.

Beat.

Yasmin   uncle knows I'm here today?

Raheel (*nods*)   yeah, he's texting, keeps in touch with me, looking out for me, int he?

Yasmin   so, what else is he saying?

Raheel   . . .

Yasmin   about me?

Raheel   . . .

Yasmin   tell me . . .

Raheel   . . .

Yasmin   what else is he saying?

I'd love to know . . . I'm your aunty, closer than he'll ever be, tell me, what's he saying?

Raheel *takes the knife and starts to chop an apple as a distraction – calm his nerves.*

Raheel   uncle Zahir's friends they were like, kinda, calling women like you 'Stellas' was weird and they were sayin' sayin' that you're women who drink, who spill wine on your tops . . .

Yasmin   !!!

Yasmin   which friends!?

Raheel   these new guys they've come from out of the city, to help us, seem to know uncle really well / and.

Yasmin   these . . . these . . . New Dawn lot!? Sofia's new friends!?

Raheel *nods.*

Yasmin (*crushed*)   I should've known . . .

Raheel   Islam provides women with all their rights . . . uncle said . . . these brothers, they were saying . . .

Yasmin   so, where are they then? these rights . . .?

Raheel   uncle Zahir was saying today / how the . . .

Yasmin   I'm not going to listen to what your uncle Zahir has to say about women's rights, Raheel. it's your nana, and our thaya, bust a gut building that shop with 'their bare hands', not him, they're the real heroes and he, your uncle, got given it, just like that; after he'd already started one family, dumped her, moved on to another, so he has a cheek parading around, preaching as if he's some paragon of virtue . . .

Beat.

none of them care about girls not this New – slash – 'prehistoric' Dawn, nor those EDL Neanderthals, not the police, not the services, and they're *paid* a wage to look after them . . . none of them did anything, did they? to stop this horror . . . none of them . . . speak to Jade.

bless her . . .

Raheel   he turned his life round . . . didn't he? uncle?

Yasmin   he hasn't even left his childhood home, Raheel!

Raheel   . . .

Yasmin   y'know, Raheel, when me and your mum were little, that shop it belonged to all of us; we'd run through the aisles playing 'chase' . . . and I'd always lose . . . even though your mum was slower . . . I'd always lose, cos I'd just stop at the dahls, transfixed at all them colours, don't get me started on all the spices . . . the reds n yellows n browns . . . do you notice all the differing colours, all the varied reds and all the shapes – it's like sunshine when I think of them times.

Raheel   notice how the boxes are heavy, make my arms hurt.

Yasmin   come, Raheel, to Manchester – let's get away from all this for a while, at least till it dies down . . .

Raheel   I'm needed here, best stick with [our own]

Yasmin   we're own, me and Jamal, remember . . . your DNA, no one will ever take that away from us.

Raheel   . . .

Yasmin   . . .

Raheel   but this is where family is, shouldn't it be you and Jamal coming back here.

Yasmin   are you sure they'd let us . . .?

Raheel   they will, they will . . . you know they will . . .

Yasmin   I'm not so sure . . .

Beat.

can Jamal bring his boyfriend? ask uncle that . . .

Raheel   !!

Yasmin   yes, Raheel . . .

Raheel   whoa! Jamal!?

Yasmin   yep his boyfriend Izan, that's who he's staying with at the moment . . . we've had an argument but he wants you to know, he wants you all to know . . . so will uncle and all his friends take Jamal and Izan to the mosque? will they? will the men embrace him and Izan? oh and could I go to the mosque, Raheel, and not have to go through the back door with all the women; have those rubbish toilets, y'know us, with with our periods, carrying babies, would we be able to have the bigger, better toilets that the men have? I would love to be here, with my sister, my family, all of them – I would love it, if only, but those double standards, Raheel . . . like your uncle's blaming your mum for what happened to you and Jade – that's just sick!

Raheel   . . .

Yasmin   . . .

Raheel   I'll be in my room, khala. . .

He is still holding the knife that he has stopped cutting an apple with.

Yasmin   be careful of that knife I've sharpened it . . .

Raheel *puts the knife down.*

Exits.

Scene Two

Later.

Yasmin *has tidied the kitchen and is now sitting, waiting, with her coat on.* **Zara** *and* **Sofia** *have just entered.*

Lights up.

Zara *wearily takes her coat off.*

Zara   charged them with violent disorder, Yas . . . ten of them, ten of our men!

Beat.

Sofia   kettled – khala! they were kettled . . .

Yasmin *shakes her head.*

Sofia   kettled! only three EDL arrested, n they threw bricks! tried to set the mosque on fire! only three can y'believe it, khala! and we were kettled . . .

Yasmin   what?!!

Sofia   'Forestdale Rape Capital of Britain' – that's what they've spray-painted – on the town hall . . . three of them, ten of ours.

Zara   it's Mohammed Ilyas, from school, Fiaz Bhatt, Iftikhar, Yas!

Yasmin   no! our lads . . .

Zara   Tariq Iqbal . . . Shafaq khan . . . I could cry . . .

Yasmin   . . .

Sofia   but, khala, amma she stood up . . . and . . . and shouted stuff dint ya? shouted, after this policeman said their names. please do it mum, do it for khala please?

Zara   all I said, Yas, all I said was . . . that he's a warehouse worker, a delivery driver, a manager, he's a lecturer, he is a market trader, we're social workers, teachers, drivers . . . ten men, ten jobs, innocent men arrested for nothing, one old innocent man murdered, one young man falsely accused . . .

Sofia   at least one, mum!

Zara   stop demonising us, these law-abiding members of our community, Forestdale community, members of this country.

Yasmin   you say that, Zara?!

Sofia   mum did!

Zara   we been here all our lives, Yas, and, still we have to say this!

Sofia   everyone's got criminals ant they, khala? every community. not just us, why do they treat us like we're *all* criminals . . . I wanna say: you know us . . . you know who we are . . . don't ya? why you doing this to us? why aren't we 'innocent till proven guilty' same as you?

Yasmin   . . .

Zara   . . .

Sofia   we've organised this meeting – 8pm, khala – gives time for people to get here, people are coming from all over.

Yasmin   finally getting organised, ey?

Sofia   people kept saying there's no smoke without fire, but it's not our fire is it, khala? it's like we're just choking on all the fumes . . .

Zara *notices* **Yasmin** *has her coat on:*

Zara   you're not staying, Yas?

Yasmin   seems like everything's in hand, Zara.

(*To* **Sofia** *as she hugs her goodbyes:*)   you and Raheel should come over to us – get a break from all this.

Sofia (*hugs her aunt back*)   thanks for coming, khala, love to Jamal.

Yasmin (*to* **Zara**)   Raheel's not himself, you need to keep an eye.

Zara (*to* **Sofia**)   remember what I said . . .

Sofia   yeah my coursework . . . I know . . .

Sofia *leaves to exit upstairs* (*and not do her homework*).

Zara (*shouting to* **Sofia**)   get that done, if you want to go to that meeting later, n stay off that twitter . . . please.

Sofia (*offstage*)   I know!

still gotta get the word out tho . . .

Zara (*to* **Sofia**)   don't post till we know more details, that's what they said . . .

Sofia (*offstage*)   I know!

Beat.

Zara (*to* **Yasmin**)   you said you took the week off?

Yasmin   not sure I'm helping ya, Zara . . .

Zara   this meeting tonight . . . your experience, be good –
you should stay . . .

Yasmin   weather's turning n all, so best off.

Zara   stay for the khatham, Yasmin . . . you did do the
chopping for it . . .

Yasmin *shrugs.*

Zara   thanks for sorting me kitchen.

Yasmin   hope it helps ya, Zara . . .

Zara   Yasmin?

Yasmin *attempts to hand a £20 note to* **Zara**. **Zara** *doesn't take it:*

Yasmin   here, stick that in the fundraiser . . .

and, y'know, phone Jade . . .

She hugs **Zara**. **Zara** *is reticent.*

Yasmin   see ya . . .

Yasmin *attempts to exit through the back door again.*

Zara   y'not blaming me are ya? for the mess *here* [in my
home]

Yasmin *stops in her tracks.*

Zara   are you? are you? blaming me?

Yasmin   I'm not blaming ya . . . juss y'know, need to see
my son.

Yasmin *trying to exit.*

Zara   how was she? Jade?

Yasmin   okay . . . on the outside. just call her, Zara, she
doesn't blame you either . . . okay?

Yasmin *attempts to leave again.*

Zara   why did Jamal stop coming?

Yasmin   for starters, got sick of 'em down that shop, dropping change from a distance, tired of being treated like a pariah / and, Zara [Jamal's gay]

Zara   they're just idiots, Yas, y'know what they're like.

Yasmin   I know how he feels . . .

Zara   what's that supposed to mean . . .?
things I do for you, I've done for ya, Yas?
you know that, don't ya
stick up for you whenever Zahir / starts about

Yasmin   oh yes Zahir! he's filling Raheel's head with crap calling me a Stella / and you're letting him . . .

Zara   he was here. he stepped in. he's his uncle.

Yasmin   and what about his aunty ey? your sister – not your cousin. wake up, Zara! you'd rather have this abuser Sajid here, you'd rather have him here, chat with him, than me!

Zara's *asthma is triggered.*

Zara (*struggling with her asthma*)   you left!!! you left, Zara!

Yasmin   because I had to! y'know I had to! /

Zara   one day, you were just gone! / gone!

Yasmin   I had no choice!
they hate me
have I hurt anyone, raped, beaten anyone /

Zara   have *I*?!

Yasmin   I'm treated like [shit] like, like I've got a disease or something . . . all I wanted was to be . . . was to be . . . [accepted]

Zara *still struggling with her asthma:*

Yasmin   they say don't they, a child will burn down the village to feel its warmth . . .

Beat.

so I better go . . .

Yasmin *attempts to leave again.*

Zara   no, Yas, you don't [understand]
what I'm [holding]
you left! gone! just like that!
where were you?
when I needed you!
where were you?

Yasmin   you don't want me here . . . do ya?

Zara (*breathless*)   I . . . do . . .

Finally **Yasmin** *realises the state that* **Zara** *is in. She jumps into sisterly action.*

Yasmin   shit!

She runs around looking for **Zara**'s *inhaler:*

Zara (*gasping*)   I do, I do . . . Yas, don't go like this again . . .

Yasmin   where the fuck is it?

Finds the inhaler, ensures that **Zara** *has taken it. Just as this happens – another knock at the door:*

Jade   Aunty Zara! Aunty Yasmin!

Loud knocking.

Aunty Zara! Aunty Yasmin!

Yasmin   [non verbally – I've got to open it].

Zara   [non verbally – please – no!]

Yasmin, *determined, exits to the front –* **Zara** *finds a place to conceal herself as in the beginning.*

Yasmin – *offstage – opens the front door.*

Voices *heard offstage.*

Jade   is she back now? Aunty Zara?

Yasmin   no. sorry, Jade, still out.

Jade *barges into the kitchen.* **Zara** *is still hidden and unseen by* **Jade**.

Jade   still?

Yasmin   sorry . . .

Jade   what about Raheel? he must be back.

Yasmin   it's not a good time now.

Jade   I just wanna put things right . . .

Yasmin   he's a bit shaken, juss give him time . . .

Jade   brought the apology from page 8.

She hands the clipping from The Chronicle.

can you see it? type's a bit small.

Beat.

can *I* give it to him?

Yasmin   I'll give it him. I will. thanks, Jade.

Jade   what am I gonna say tomorrow?

Yasmin   ?

Jade   this publisher? book deal? told ya it's happening tomorrow . . .

Yasmin   I dunno . . .

Baby starts crying a slight distance away:

that's Jaden, in the car – my friend gave me a lift – kinda sprang it on her . . .

Jade, *completely deflated, attempts to leave:*

thanks – I won't bother again . . .

Yasmin   wait! Jade! wait!

Jade *returns.*

Yasmin   you said . . . something about this other girl from
primary school . . . what . . . what is it you meant . . .?

Jade   yeah, I was there at those parties, and she was so little
. . . didn't have her salwar on . . . and . . . and . . . no one
knows where she is . . . and . . . never mind . . .

Yasmin   does Zara know about this?

Jade   think so – that's why this book [it's so important] –

oh nevermind. thanks anyway.

Baby cries louder. **Jade***'s gone.*

Yasmin *wants to go after her. Realises it's hopeless without* **Zara***'s
collaboration.*

Yasmin *returns.*

Yasmin   see – I'm not helping, am I?

wish I could help, Zara . . .

I wish . . .

Zara   you are, Yas, you are . . .

Slight pause as **Yasmin** *considers. Acknowledges her sister in a
heap on the floor.*

Yasmin *takes her outdoor shoes off, puts on a pair of* **Zara***'s
slippers/indoor shoes.*

Yasmin *then approaches her sister's CD collection. Looks through
this collection. Chooses a CD. Puts it in the CD player. Presses
play: Iqbal Bano singing Faiz Ahmed Faiz's 'Hum Dekhenge' plays.*

Zara   Iqbal Bano's version . . .?

Yasmin   of course – who else ey?

Beat.

beautiful int it?

The sisters listen for a bit.

Yasmin   I was never like you . . .

Zara   I was never like you, that cig I had that day n I vomited.

Yasmin   I know, it was only a berkley menthol n all.

They catch each others' eyes:

Yasmin   y'need to speak this:

She turns the music off / down.

Zara   sometimes. some things are [just unspeakable . . .]

Yasmin   but we must, Zara, we must. bring it in the open
. . .

Zara *takes a deep breath:*

Zara   this Sajid turns up out of the blue – gave him a bit of work, kitchen, here, needed sorting . . . and yeah, I fed him, once or twice, it's what we do, don't we? feed each other, that's all, I had no idea – how d'y'know, Yas?

Yasmin   was there something going on, Zara?

Zara   no, course there wasn't!

Yasmin   . . . sure?

Zara   there *wasn't*.

Yasmin   did you want there to be?

Zara   no, I didn't, course I didn't. I didn't.

Beat.

it was *Jade* he came for. she was always round 'ere. he was round 'ere. then *she* just stopped coming. he disappeared. how did I not think . . .?

Beat.

soon as I heard what he'd done . . . got rid of every trace.

Yasmin   . . .

Zara   dismantled everything, whole kitchen – threw it out in a skip. but . . . it's the same room, Yas. can't change it.

Yasmin   you heard her, just now – you heard her, she wants to help . . .

Zara   how can *she* help?

Yasmin   all the stuff with Raheel, all the stuff going on round here . . .

Zara   damage is done, Yas.

Beat.

Yasmin   ya started the women's centre, dint ya, to get some of the house-bound women out . . . help them with English, Quranic lessons, cooking and . . .

Zara   all the crap comes to me – you scratch the surface, try and help and . . . /

Yasmin   crap always comes . . . but what you did wasn't crap, was it?

Slight pause.

Yasmin   what does Jade mean about this primary school girl?

where is she, Zara?

Pause.

Zara   it was this little apnee girl, first I knew about all this – 'a sexual health worker' – goree – comes to see me one day . . . all puffed up with herself – tells me it was disclosed, a little kid, young as nine or ten, had been at one of those 'parties'. witness statement said she was . . . 'raped up her arse to protect her honour'? – could I clarify this for her . . .

Yasmin   !!!

Zara   I starts saying kalmey in my head, cos believe, Yas, I was mad – politely and calmly I said: 'isn't this your remit, child sexual exploitation . . .?' she didn't say anything . . . I said, 'it's not part of any culture or community is it, so you explain this to me'. I waited and I said it again . . . 'you explain it . . . isn't *your* remit CSE . . .?' tumbleweed . . . so I said, 'so where is she now, this little girl, exactly . . .?' she had no clue. told me her friends from school were saying she went missing after school on friday, her dad, he called the police, then she was dropped off monday morning . . .

Yasmin   taken from school?!

Zara   school playground, after the weekend, she was just shoved back into the playground, just like that.

Slight pause as **Yasmin** *absorbs the horror of this:*

Zara   not one of them, not one of them, school, police, social services, did anything.

Yasmin   but where is she now? this little girl?

Zara   Pakistan, Yas.

Yasmin   fuck.

Zara   now . . . you know . . .

Yasmin   . . .

Zara   . . .

Yasmin   Zara, this has to come out. it has to.

Zara   no, Yas, it can't.

Yasmin   we have to act on this . . .

Zara   no, Yas, we can't.

Yasmin   look, we've got a campaign, we're getting organised for the men, everyone's mobilising, n people speaking out / so, what about this little girl and all the other girls we don't know about!?

Zara   Yasmin, this is why I can't talk to you / why I can't talk to you!

Yasmin   why are we expendable, Zara? us women and girls? why! I can't bear it . . .

Zara   Yasmin, listen, we have to work discreetly, don't you get it?

Yasmin   I see that, of course I see that . . . y'know I see that /

Zara   it's dangerous – for these girls . . . imagine, Yas, this getting out, the media twisting it, like they do, like they have, blaming us all, arresting innocents . . .

Yasmin   but we have to do something, don't we? Zara?

Zara   . . .

Yasmin   we have to, we have to . . . we have to tell the story of this little apnee girl, we'll ask, we'll find out about any other girls, we don't know about, we'll slowly, diligently, tell their stories . . . her, others and . . . and . . . and . . .

Zara   and what, Yasmin? and then what? who's going to listen to us, we're used to dealing with this shit on our own, aren't we?

Yasmin   we amplify . . .

there's others aren't there? other groups, organisations isn't there . . . there's Roshni, isn't there? Himmet, Apna Haq, c'mon who else . . . c'mon who else, Zara . . .? who else?

Zara   !

Yasmin   c'mon, Zara . . . who else? they'll help, we'll do it together . . . think about it . . . others, together . . . all of us . . . trust me on this, Zara! trust me, Zara, I am *your* sister:

Beat.

Zara (*conceding*)   Saheli, Sharan, loads of Roshnis up and down the country . . .

Yasmin   all we have to do is ask . . . no one ever asks us, do they? they'll help.

Beat.

and Jade.

Yasmin *picks up* **Jade***'s number and passes it to* **Zara**. **Zara** *is reluctant.*

Yasmin   she'll help, she really wants to . . .

Zara   . . .

Yasmin   I'm here . . . you can do it . . . you have to . . . you, sorry, 'we' *we* have to, *we have to* – Zara.

Zara *takes the slip of paper. A deep breath. She gets out her phone and starts dialling.* **Yasmin** *puts it on speaker to support.*

Enter **Sofia** *with her laptop. Hears* **Jade***'s answerphone:*

Jade (*answerphone*)   'hi it's Jade Steel, can't get to the phone right now, leave your name n number and I'll get right back'.

Sofia   mum! you phoning Jade!!!

Zara *cuts the call.*

Sofia   you can't phone Jade, mum!

Zara   I know, Sofia! I know!

Sofia   mum, y'know what they'll do, you know what they'll do: they'll print – we've got a grooming factory in the house!!!

Zara   we're gonna have to speak to her sometime, Sofia, can't avoid her forever.

Sofia   but uncle said we're best to stay out of trouble.

Zara   trouble is here, it's already here.

Sofia   but everyone's unfriended me as it is!

Enter **Raheel**.

Sofia (*to* **Raheel**)   mum's phoning Jade, Raheel! mum's phoning Jade, can y'believe it . . .

Yasmin   she just wants to help; she's brought the apology they printed . . . look . . .

Zara *shows them the clipping. They look.* **Raheel** *grabs it, tries to absorb it.*

Zara   she could help clear your brother's name? think about it.

Sofia   page 8, tho and it's tiny . . .

Yasmin   it's a start!

Sofia   look at what's happened.

Yasmin   it's not your mum's fault is it! or Jade's or *yours* is it? any of this . . .

Sofia   mum . . . uncle said – he and New Dawn, they can help with this.

Yasmin   not Zahir again!!

Sofia   it's in the 'strategic plan'.

Yasmin   my head hurts.

Sofia   the female branch of New Dawn, we can work with you, improve communication and *cohesion*.

Yasmin   what?

Sofia   improve communication and cohesion . . . the female branch.

Beat.

Yasmin   so, who's in this female branch then?

Sofia (*proud*)   me –

Yasmin   !

Sofia   New Dawn can get funding for me to work with them for real . . . run the female branch and – get this! – then I can stay here, not go to uni, help you develop your centre! you could be part of all this! think about it, it'll be a win-win for all of us, mum!

Beat.

Zara   I dunno, Sofia, I dunno . . . I have to protect the women, the wives of the accused, their kids are going hungry and . . .

Sofia   uncle can help with food and deliveries – y'know he can . . .

Zara   those women, they won't leave their houses cos they're so ashamed . . .

Beat.

think about it, Sofia, it's fragile isn't it, our space . . . can't just let anyone in . . .

Raheel   who are these New Dawn guys? they're not from round here are they, Sofia?

Sofia   they're our brothers, they've come all this way to support / us!

Raheel   it's like uncle's been brainwashed by them.

Sofia   uncle is New Dawn, he's community leader!

Raheel   but who's he leading? from the community?

Sofia   me – it's just the start!

Yasmin   but what do they stand for, Sofe? that's all we're asking . . .

Sofia   for us to not be treated like this! it's obvious.

Yasmin   but think about it, think about it, why do they wanna move in on yer mum's patch?

Beat.

Sofia (*determined*)   I've not explained this right, have I?

She tries new tactics and opens her laptop:

Reading from her website:

it's really good, listen

'at New Dawn we work to redress the bias, distortion and Islamophobia that leads to Muslims being portrayed in the media as one-dimensional, othered, sometimes violent and deviant . . .'

Raheel   . . .

Zara   you write that, Sofe?

Sofia *nods with pride.*

Sofia   we're working to reframe the narrative, aren't we? – getting our side across – listen: why is the race of white perpetrators never emphasised by mainstream media? it's mainly white European males in their mid-forties, making extensive use of the internet for grooming. what happens to those victims if the focus is mainly on Asian grooming gangs?

Yasmin (*moves towards the laptop, impressed*)   you research all this, Sofe?

Sofia *pulls the laptop away.*

Yasmin   this – the website?

Sofia   just a draft.

Yasmin   nice design – what's that next bit say?

Sofia   Mosim, Tahir, Moz wrote that . . .

Raheel (*rolls his eyes*)   them lot!

Yasmin   [bingo!] Mosim, Tahir and Moz . . . aaah . . . they're not in the female branch are they?

Sofia   no, they're the founders – have to run everything by them is all –

Yasmin   scroll down a bit.

Sofia   don't read that bit / it's not finished

Yasmin   Sofe?

Sofia *is reticent.* **Yasmin**, *determined, scrolls:*

Yasmin   [bingo!] (*reads*) 'we at "New Dawn" call upon all media including news outlets to immediately cease portrayals of our men as misogynistic in any way, and our females as oppressed by their male counterparts'.

Zara   ay! hay! my head hurts!

Raheel   mine too.

Sofia   portrayals of our men as misogynistic – is weaponised against us . . . isn't it?

Yasmin   don't this New Dawn and Zahir want us to talk about misogyny?

Sofia   cos like I said it's weaponised against us, I mean look at today . . . what's happened to our men . . .

Beat.

Yasmin   how else did all this happen though? all this abuse . . . come on, Sofe, agree misogyny is weaponised, but that shouldn't silence us.

Sofia   you don't live here, khala! d'ya?

Yasmin   do you know what's going on the world over for women and girls?

Sofia   so, what do you know about it?

Beat.

Raheel   whoa!

Yasmin   if they really gave a shit about misogyny and this 'weaponising' why didn't they say: stop the hyper-focus on just Muslims – like the men today – bring the focus back on the girls and women – Big. Full. Stop!

Sofia   you've no idea what it's been like for us!

Raheel   whoa!

Sofia   you, you, you do this big empowerment schtick, don't ya! uncle was saying . . . it's vulgarity as empowerment / . . .

Yasmin (*sits*)   Zara, you know what – I might need one them herbal teas now!

Sofia   because, because you've had to lose your roots haven't ya?!! /

Zara   Sofia!

Raheel   shit!

Zara   do you want a ginseng and mango, Yasmin?

Yasmin   these friends of yours . . . this 'Archaic Dawn' – wake up, Sofe, they're just cavemen in cahoots with all the other knuckle-draggers – two cheeks of the same arse, ennit!

Zara   Yas!

Raheel *sniggers.*

Zara   Raheel!

Yasmin   what do you think, Raheel?

Raheel   er . . .

Yasmin   say it – what you think – about this statement?

Beat.

Raheel   bit you wrote 'bout Muslims in the media, that bits good, but sorry, Sofe . . . 'cease portrayals of our men as misogynistic' from those guys that were chatting shit in the shop today . . . sounds well dodgy . . .

Sofia   whose side are you on, Raheel? doing this for you!

Raheel I'm on your side! – Sofia, it could've been you!

Beat.

Zara (*puts her head in her hands*)   no!

Her asthma is triggered.

Yasmin Zara?

Zara *finds her asthma pump and inhales.*

Yasmin *observes her sister and realises she needs to back off a bit.*

Sofia *and* **Raheel** *are speechless.*

Beat.

Zara (*to her children*)   what's happened ey? where are all your friends!?

Sofia New Dawn are my friends!

Zara no, no your friends – your real friends?

Sofia stopped getting in touch dint they? real friends are meant to stand by yer . . .

Zara (*holds her phone out*)   give 'em a call . . .

Sofia I did, mum, they haven't got back to me . . .

Zara I'll ring 'em then.

She goes to call.

Sofia stop it, mum! stop it!

I don't care about them, I don't care about Iram, Saira and Shaheen, they ignore me at the bus stop, sit behind me in class and . . . and . . . I want to stay here with you – I don't want to be at uni on my own . . . and . . . and . . . forget it . . . who listens to me anyway . . .

She gives up and focuses on her work on the ND website.

Zara *puts her phone down.*

Raheel (*deflated*)   sorry, Sofe, is it cos of *me*?

Yasmin *and* **Zara** *notice both the children's anguish and look at each other.*

Zara   but you're not on your own? never!

Sofia   I'm busy, mum, don't worry about me. . .

Yasmin's *mobile interrupts, she answers the call.*

Yasmin   hi, Jamal, I'm so glad you've called back, but

Pause.

yeah yeah, here with them all now – best I call you later /

Raheel   can I speak with him, Jamal . . . can I speak to him?

Yasmin   hang on . . .

Yasmin *gives the phone to* **Raheel**.

Raheel   hey, bruv, no, you're not on speaker . . .

yeah, yeah, yeah,

Beat.

I didn't have anything to do with anything

kasme, bro

you believe me?

there's an apology printed today

Pause.

really?

Pause.

it's been mad, crazy shit

yeah, yeah, I'll call you later . . .

Pause.

I know as well . . .

Izan . . . is it?

your boyfriend.

Beat.

Zara   !

Sofia   [what?!]

Raheel *looking at* **Yasmin**. **Yasmin** *nods but avoids* **Zara**'s *eyes.*

Raheel   it's cool, bro . . . totally cool . . . I mean truth . . .

I'll call you later.

safe.

He hands the phone back to **Yasmin**.

Awkward silence as the family absorbs this new revelation about Jamal.

Zara's *text pings . . . she checks her phone . . . 'thanks for the onions'* –

Zara   oh!! the khatham!! the khatham!!

She looks at **Yasmin**.

Yasmin   it's all right – off you go . . .

Zara   Nasreen's mum's beyji . . .

Yasmin   just go, Zara . . . I'll be on my way as well.

Sofia   I'll drive us, amma

Yasmin (*to* **Sofia**)   I'll spread the word . . . my ends for the Forestdale Ten . . . rally support . . . okay?

Yasmin *hugs her niece.*

Beat.

Zara *and* **Sofia** *both put on their coats and headscarves.*

Zara   y'can drive us, can't ya, Yas?

Sofia   mum! I'll drive! I can drive now, mum

Zara   alright, Sofia!

(*To* **Yasmin**.) y'can't do snakes pass at this time? yer got yer overnight bag, so yer gonna come . . .

Yasmin   how about I come back once you've had a chance to speak to Jade, ey?

Zara   Yas, we can't part like this, y'should stay . . .

Yasmin   need to see my boy, Zara . . .

Beat.

Zara   he's welcome, he'll always be welcome.

Yasmin *hugs* **Zara** – *this means the world.*

Yasmin   come over to us will ya

Zara *nods.*

Zara *passes* **Sofia** *the car keys, as they exit.*

Sofia   we're going to khala's? you said from time we're not allowed to go to khala's . . .

Zara *gently hits* **Sofia** *as if to say be quiet.*

Zara *and* **Sofia** *leave to go to the khatham and then the meeting.*

Yasmin (*to* **Raheel**)   you be alright?

Raheel *nods.*

Yasmin   what you did then – on the phone – with everyone listening as well – it'll mean a lot to him that, you don't know . . .

Raheel   just did it

Yasmin *goes to exit.*

Beat.

Raheel   can I ask . . .?

Yasmin   anything . . .

Raheel   how did you do it, out there, on your own?

Beat.

Yasmin   faith, that's how y'know in my work . . . social
work, I see a lot – people in the worst of circumstances, and
when you see that, those people fighting to survive another
day – real faith is getting up to fight another day . . . I had
faith, out there, on my own, something was looking after me,
no matter what: after all 'Bismillahir Rahmanir Raheem . . .
it means: 'Allah is the most beneficent and the most merciful'
– don't it?

Beat.

you know where I am.

She exits.

Fade to black.

Scene Three

Later.

*After the khatham, and the campaign meeting for the Forestdale
Ten.* **Zara**'s *kitchen.*

Lights up just after **Zara** *and* **Sofia** *have returned taking their
coats off:*

Sofia   Raheel! Raheel!

Zara   your khala, she gone?

Enter **Raheel**.

Raheel *nods.*

Zara *(sighs)*   she never stays. know what she's like!

She hands a reused ice cream tub full of palak to **Raheel**.

Zara   Aunty Nas's palak . . .

Raheel   thanks. how was the meeting?

Sofia   people came from all over: London, Stoke-on Trent, Milton Keynes . . . these lawyers, Raheel, from the 'Fletcher, Reed, and Khan' campaigns. it was really good: we held 'a vote of no confidence in the police' – can y'believe that!

Raheel   really?

Sofia   unanimous, Raheel! unanimous!

Raheel   [wow!]

Beat.

Raheel   uncle – was he at the meeting?

Sofia   yeah he was.

Zara   he still not message you back?

Raheel *shakes his head.*

Raheel   cos I won't go to the ND meeting tomorrow . . .

Zara *shakes her head.*

Sofia   there was this goree there, Raheel, she's giving us money, she thinks ND are great.

Zara (*sarcastic*)   well, there's an endorsement.

Beat.

he looked really out of his depth tonight . . .

Sofia   yeah, but it was us at New Dawn who set it up that meeting. wouldn't have all come together without them, uncle and me, would it?

Raheel   we'd've set it up, us lot – if they arrest people for nothing. we'd've done it! look at everything you and mum did today, Sofe. dint need them, they just took over dint they?

Sofia   no they didn't!

Zara, *wanting to placate her children, gets some onions and hands an onion each to* **Raheel** *and* **Sofia***:*

Zara   here – c'mon now . . . can ya help me peel? let's batch cook tomorrow morning . . . so I can have the rest of the week off!

there's going to be changes round here . . . there is . . .

Beat.

c'mon . . .

Raheel *and* **Sofia** *both reluctantly start peeling:* **Zara** *sniffs the onion.*

Zara   smell that, it's good to peel . . .. piyazz, thom . . . I love it . . . back to my real roots

c'mon, smell . . .

Raheel *and* **Sofia** *nonchalantly sniff.*

The three of them peel.

Raheel   mum, I want a proper break from all this – like khala said.

Zara   agree.

Sofia   a break – like a holiday?!

Zara   a break – like a break.

Sofia   what about Dubai mum? Iram went there last year. she loved it, they've got supermalls /

Zara   I was actually thinking Manchester . . .

Sofia   Manchester!! honestly, mum, dint think khala had got to you that bad . . . holidaying in Manchester! whoa, the world has turned on its axis badly.

Zara   no one will recognise him there, and Jamal's there too . . . be nice to meet this Izan won't it?

it's a 'win-win' for us all, Raheel going to Manchester . . .
while it settles here . . .

Sofia   what about uncle, mum?

Zara   I'll deal with uncle, don't you worry about that.

Her phone pings, she looks:

oh. she can't do the outfits . . . tailor . . . this Mariam.

Raheel   cos of me ennit . . .

Zara   no, too late notice, Raheel . . . here, dig your nails in
. . .

Raheel *and* **Sofia** *attempt to dig their nails in:*

Zara   focus on all the layers and peeling them back.

She tries a different tack to soothe her children and approaches her CD player. She looks at her CD collection.

y'know when me, your khala, when we were your age
we'd be listening to tunes, dancing n dressing up in our
bedroom . . .

She puts on a CD: 'Back To Life' by Soul II Soul plays.

Zara *starts to strut some 80s moves: Butterfly, Running Man, MC ammer, etc., around* **Raheel** *and* **Sofia**. **Raheel** *and* **Sofia** *are mortified at this mum-dancing.*

Raheel *makes out he can't watch, he laughs, puts his arms over his eyes:*

Zara (*to* **Raheel**)   come, dance with your mum for a bit . . .

She grabs **Sofia** *and* **Raheel** *and attempts to spin them around. They both giggle and half-heartedly attempt to resist their mum's advances.*

Sofia   seriously, mum!!

There's a sudden loud knocking on the front door. The music is switched off. They all freeze.

Jade (*offstage*)   Aunty Zara!

Aunty Zara!

you there?

Zara *looks at her children, and looks towards the front door.*

Beat.

Jade   Aunty Zara!

Zara   come round the back, Jade, it's open.

End.

Methuen Drama Modern Plays

include

Bola Agbaje
Edward Albee
Ayad Akhtar
Jean Anouilh
John Arden
Peter Barnes
Sebastian Barry
Clare Barron
Alistair Beaton
Brendan Behan
Edward Bond
William Boyd
Bertolt Brecht
Howard Brenton
Amelia Bullmore
Anthony Burgess
Leo Butler
Jim Cartwright
Lolita Chakrabarti
Caryl Churchill
Lucinda Coxon
Tim Crouch
Shelagh Delaney
Ishy Din
Claire Dowie
David Edgar
David Eldridge
Dario Fo
Michael Frayn
John Godber
James Graham
David Greig
John Guare
Lauren Gunderson
Peter Handke
David Harrower
Jonathan Harvey
Robert Holman
David Ireland
Sarah Kane

Barrie Keeffe
Jasmine Lee-Jones
Anders Lustgarten
Duncan Macmillan
David Mamet
Patrick Marber
Martin McDonagh
Arthur Miller
Alistair McDowall
Tom Murphy
Phyllis Nagy
Anthony Neilson
Peter Nichols
Ben Okri
Joe Orton
Vinay Patel
Joe Penhall
Luigi Pirandello
Stephen Poliakoff
Lucy Prebble
Peter Quilter
Mark Ravenhill
Philip Ridley
Willy Russell
Jackie Sibblies Drury
Sam Shepard
Martin Sherman
Chris Shinn
Wole Soyinka
Simon Stephens
Kae Tempest
Anne Washburn
Laura Wade
Theatre Workshop
Timberlake Wertenbaker
Roy Williams
Snoo Wilson
Frances Ya-Chu Cowhig
Benjamin Zephaniah

For a complete listing of
Methuen Drama titles, visit:
www.bloomsbury.com/drama

Follow us on Twitter and keep up to date
with our news and publications
@MethuenDrama